THE

HISTORY AND PHILOSOPHY

OF

MARRIAGE;

OR,

POLYGAMY AND MONOGAMY COMPARED.

BY A CHRISTIAN PHILANTHROPIST.

"There shall be no widows in the land, for I will marry them all; there shall be no orphans, for I will father them all."

— OLD PLAY.

Born Again Publishing, Inc.

Polygamy and Monogamy

I have in my library a copy of *Polygamy and Monogamy*. At least that's the title on the cover. On the spine it says *History and Philosophy of Marriage* and on the title page it says, *The History and Philosophy of Marriage or Polygamy and Monogamy Compared*. To simplify things, I've chosen to use the title that's displayed on the cover; Polygamy and Monogamy. In addition to the title discrepancy, the original author left off his name and inserted the following: BY A CHRISTIAN PHILANTHROPIST. As a result of the absence of an author's name, many readers mistook the publisher for the author. This new version of the previous work has a new publisher so that error won't be perpetuated. Finally, this new book has a new copyright due to the fact that it is a compilation of images. The pages that you see here are photographs of the original pages with appropriate corrections to the ink smudges and missing typeset. Because of the amount of editing necessary to make the pages readable, each page is as unique as a finger print. Copyright infringers, you have been warned.

Polygamy

AND

Monogamy

INVOCATION.

———◆———

I HAVE chosen an "adventurous" theme, — the philosophy of the great passion, an analysis of the primary laws of marriage, and an examination and comparison of antagonistic systems of social life, —

"Things unattempted yet in prose or rhyme.

And chiefly thou, O Spirit, that dost prefer
Before all temples th' upright heart and pure,
Instruct me, for thou know'st : thou from the first
Wast present, and, with mighty wings outspread,
Dove-like sat'st brooding on the vast abyss,
And mad'st it pregnant.   What in me is dark,
Illumine! what is low, raise and support!
That to the height of this great argument
I may assert eternal providence,
And justify the ways of God to men."

Publisher's Advertisement.

Opinions of Eminent Literary Men.

Of Notices received from Competent Judges to whom this work has been submitted we insert the following: —

FROM THE HON. G. W. CURTIS, M.A.,
Professor of Recent Literature in Cornell University.

I have read the proof-sheets of "THE HISTORY AND PHILOSOPHY OF MARRIAGE," in which the author treats a very difficult and delicate subject with knowledge, candor, and evident honesty of purpose. It is the contribution of an argument, usually wholly unconsidered, to the discussion of a question which challenges the grave attention of civilization, and which Mr. Lecky treats in his recent "History of European Morals," reaching, however, a conclusion directly opposed to that of this little work. This book has the curious distinction of being a Christian plea for polygamy. I do not agree with its conclusions; but I cannot quarrel with its spirit.

GEORGE WILLIAM CURTIS.

JULY 9, 1869.

FROM F. B. SANBORN, M.A.,
Associate Editor of the Springfield Republican.

The author of "THE HISTORY AND PHILOSOPHY OF MARRIAGE" some time since submitted his manuscript to my examination, and I have read, with interest, the greater part of the work. It advances opinions with which I cannot agree ; and these are based upon premises that I should very much question; but as the expression of a sincere conviction founded on extensive observation and reading, it seems to me entitled to attention, respect, and refutation, by those competent to meet the arguments presented with other arguments, and not with mere contradiction.

F. B. SANBORN.

SPRINGFIELD, Aug. 13, 1869.

CONTENTS.

5

CHAPTER IV. — ORIGIN OF POLYGAMY.

CHAPTER V. — ORIGIN OF MONOGAMY.

CHAPTER VI. — MONOGAMY AFTER THE INTRODUCTION OF CHRISTIANITY.

CHAPTER VII. — MONOGAMY AS IT IS.

CHAPTER VIII. — RELATION OF MONOGAMY TO CRIME.

CHAPTER IX. — OBJECTIONS TO POLYGAMY.

APPENDIX. — NOTICES AND REVIEWS.

THE HISTORY

AND

PHILOSOPHY OF MARRIAGE.

CHAPTER I.

INTRODUCTORY.

AUDI ALTERAM PARTEM.

PHILOSOPHY takes nothing for granted. It doubts all things that it may prove all things. The marriage question is a proper subject of philosophical inquiry, involving an examination and analysis of both polygamy and monogamy. Of the latter form of marriage the Christian world has known too much, and of the former too little, to have felt, hitherto, the need of any analysis of either. We have inherited our monogamy, or the marriage system which restricts each man to one wife only, and have practised it as a matter of course, without any special examination or inquiry : so that we really know but little concerning its origin or its early history; while we know still less of the system of polygamy. We read something of it in the Bible and in the history of Eastern nations, and we learn something more from the reports of modern travellers ; and it cannot be denied that what we know of it has come to us in such a form as to prejudice our minds against it. This prejudice is unfavorable to a just and candid philosophical inquiry ; and while pursuing this inquiry, let us hold this prejudice in abeyance. Let us not forget that what we have seen of this system is in its most unfavorable aspects. Most travellers carry their native prejudices abroad, and look upon the customs of distant countries with less astonishment than contempt. And they remember, when writing up their accounts of those countries, that their books are made to be sold at home ; and they must not institute comparisons unfavorable to their own land, but must flatter the conceit of their fellow-countrymen by assuring them that their own social and political institutions are vastly better than those of other lands.

So, also, with history : it presents human affairs
in a perspective view, painting its roughest mountains with distinct exactness, but casting its peace-
ful plains quite into the shade.   It devotes a hundred pages to the details of wars and intrigues,
illustrating the crimes of men, in proportion to a
single page of descriptions of common life and domestic tranquillity, illustrating their virtues.

If the writer, on the contrary, shall seem preju-
diced in favor of polygamy, let it be attributed to
his love of fair play, and his desire to let both
sides be heard, rather than to any undue bias of
mind preventing him from doing equal justice to
the arguments in favor of either system.

It is attested and proved by competent authority,
which no one doubts, that polygamy, or that social
system which permits a plurality of wives, has
always prevailed in most countries and in all ages
of the world, from time immemorial ; but this
form of marriage, being foreign to the customs of
modern Europe and her colonies in America, is
very naturally regarded throughout these enlightened regions as something heathenish and barbarous.   And modern writers, whose works are the

exponents of European civilization, have hitherto
said every thing against it, and nothing for it.
But they have condemned it almost without examination or debate, rather because it is strange
than because they have proved it to be at fault.
No one has given to the subject the time and re-
search necessary to its fair elucidation. But as a
venerable institution the social system of polygamy
does not deserve such supercilious treatment.
Such treatment, besides being unjust, is unphilosoph-
ical, and unworthy a liberal and an enlightened
age. Its great antiquity alone should entitle it to
sufficient respect to be heard, at least, in its own
defence. It constitutes an important part of human history. It is a great fact that cannot be
ignored; and as such, it must be studied and
known. To insist upon the condemnation of this
system, without hearing its defence, is oppression.
It is even the worst kind of oppression; for, in such
case, it must be allied with ignorance and bigotry.
But if there ever was a time, when polygamy
could properly be thrust aside with a sneer, and it
was satisfactory to Christian justice to condemn it
unheard and unexamined, it can be so no longer;

for, with the general diffusion of knowledge and
the increased facilities of modern intercourse, our
speculative inquiries are seeking a range of cos-
mopolitan extent, and we are brought into daily
contact with the opinions and the practices of the
antipodes. If we disapprove of their practices we
should be prepared to make substantial objections
to them ; and if we wish to teach them our own,
we should be able to give equally substantial reasons. If the advocates of polygamy are in the
minority in the Christian world, let the common
rights of the minority be granted them, — freedom
of debate and the privilege of protest ; and let
their solemn protest be listened to with respect,
and be spread upon the current records of the
day. And, on the other hand, if those who practise this ancient system do constitute the majority
of mankind, it cannot be either uninteresting or
unimportant to inquire what has made it so nearly
universal, and caused it to be adopted by so many
different nations, and even different races of men,
among whom are, no doubt, some persons who are
justly distinguished for their wisdom, their piety,
and their humanity.

The writer is not aware that any former attempt has been made in this country to analyze and explain the social system of polygamy, or that any works written abroad for this purpose have ever been current here; at least, he has not been able to obtain any,* and thus to avail himself of their assistance. While, therefore, the subject-matter of this essay is of the most venerable antiquity, the manner of its discussion must be entirely new; and not only can the author claim the singular merit of originality, but the reader can be assured of the no less singular zest of novelty.

SOME ACCOUNT OF THE AUTHOR.

Almost everybody who takes up a new book is curious to know something of the writer; of his special qualifications for his work, of his opportunities of acquiring a thorough knowledge of his subject, and of the standpoint from which he views it. He will, therefore, proceed at once to give some account of himself, and how he came to write this work. And the courteous reader will now please permit him to drop the indirect style of address so

* See Appendix:

common among writers, and to introduce himself
by speaking in the first person. I am a native of
New England, and was brought up a strict Puritan.
My father always declared his intention to educate
me for the law, and I took to learning as readily
as most boys of my age. I was graduated from
college almost forty years ago, and had nearly
completed my professional studies, when my health
suddenly broke down; and I then discovered that
I had been bestowing all my care upon the improve-
ment of the mind, to the total neglect of the health-
fulness of the body. And this, I fancy, was only a
common defect at that time, in our American, or,
at least, our New-England, system of education.
The physicians having prescribed a voyage at sea
and a residence of some months in a tropical
climate, the influence of my friends obtained a foreign situation for me in one of our Boston houses
having an extensive business in India; and I became their clerk, and afterwards their factor. The
engagements then entered into could not easily be
broken off, and I have continued in them many
years; and having seen all the continents of the
globe, and many islands of the sea, and having

observed human society in every climate and in every social condition, I have at length returned to my native land, an older, and, I hope, a wiser man. Having become an active member of the church in my youth, I did not renounce my Christian character abroad, but have always afforded such encouragement and assistance as I was able, to our American and English missionaries, whenever I fell in with them. In fact, I had long cherished a profound respect and admiration for the missionary enterprise ; and, notwithstanding my father's wish to educate me for the law, I had, during my course of study, seriously offered myself as a candidate for missionary labor ; and, had I been deemed worthy of that honor, I should, no doubt, have devoted my life to that service. But Providence did not so order it. Yet when I went abroad, my early predilections easily reconciled me to the pain of leaving my native land, to the disappointment which I experienced in renouncing a career of professional and literary honors, and readily introduced me to the society of those devoted missionaries whom I would fain have chosen for my fellow-laborers and life-companions. I was very much surprised, however, soon after my first acquaintance with them, to learn that, under certain circumstances, they allowed the members of the native Christian churches a plurality of wives. As I had been educated a strict monogamist, in New England, I had never once dreamed that any other social system than monogamy could be possible among Christian people, anywhere; and I remonstrated with the missionaries for permitting polygamy among their converts, under any circumstances whatever.

WHAT THE MISSIONARIES SAY ABOUT POLYGAMY.

I was answered by them that the Bible has not forbidden it, but, on the contrary, has recognized it, as sometimes lawful and proper; and although they themselves did not encourage it, they could not positively prohibit it. I then endeavored to recollect some prohibition in the Bible, but could neither recollect nor find one there. On the contrary, to my own astonishment, after a careful examination of the Sacred Scriptures, I did find therein many things to favor it. The missionaries also said that their experience had taught them that the converting

2

grace of God was granted to those living in polygamy as often as to others; the natives themselves
attach no moral reproach to it; " and," said the
missionaries, " if such persons give evidence of
genuine conversion, ' Can any man forbid water,
that they should not be baptized, who have received
the grace of God as well as we?' Besides,"
they added, " if they are not received and recognized as Christians, how shall we dispose of them?
Shall we refuse them our fellowship, and send
them back again to their idolatry? This would be
no less unchristian than unkind. Shall we compel
them to put away all their wives, but those first
married, and then receive them into the church?
But in-many cases this would be impracticable, in
others unjust in all, cruel. For the chastity of the
women hitherto irreproachable would be tarnished
by their repudiation: they would often be left without a home and without support ; and, like other disgraced and destitute women of all lands, they would
be thrust upon a life of infamy and vice. Who,"
continued they, " shall dare assume the responsibility of separating wife from husband, and children
from parents? since the Bible expressly forbids a

man to divorce his wife, for any cause, except unfaithfulness to her marriage vow : God is not said in the Bible to hate polygamy, but it says there that ' *he hateth putting away.*' "

I need not say that I was completely disarmed and silenced by this array of " the law and the testimony ; " and was compelled, by their arguments, to admit that their course was one of equal justice and mercy. I soon learned, however, that the rules of the missionaries are by no means uniform upon this question. Many of them, particularly those who possess a great regard for the authority and the dogmas of the church, and who reason rather from the " tradition of the elders," than from the laws of Nature or of God, have rigidly enforced monogamy among their converts ; and if any one becomes a Christian while living in polygamy, such missionaries require him to repudiate all his wives but one. It was not many months after the conversation above related that one of the missionaries called my attention to a religious journal that he had just received from Boston, containing the report of certain missionaries among the North-American Indians, giving an account of the conversion of an old and influential chief.

THE INDIAN CHIEF AND HIS TWO WIVES.

This chief at the time of his conversion to Christianity was living with two wives. The one first married was now aged, blind, and childless. The other was young, attractive, healthful, and the mother of one fine boy. One of these wives the missionaries required him to put away, as an indispensable requisite to baptism and church-membership. The old chief, after careful deliberation, could not decide which one to repudiate. The first he was bound by every honorable motive " to love and to cherish," especially on account of her age and infirmity ; while the other was devotedly attached to him, and was the mother of his only child and heir, which he could not give up, and from which he could not separate the mother. He, therefore, submitted the case to the missionaries to decide which one of them he should put away. They decided against the younger one. And as he was old himself and his other wife was barren, that she must also give up her child. This mandate was obeyed with martyr-like fortitude, which nothing but the strongest religious motives could have inspired ;

opposed, as it was, to every natural sentiment of love and honor. And thus, in one hour, was that young wife and mother deprived of her husband, her child, her character, and her home; and sent away a bereaved and lonely outcast into the wide world. The report which the missionaries themselves gave of this affair closed by saying that the repudiated wife and bereaved mother soon died inconsolable and broken-hearted.

MY OWN REFLECTIONS UPON THIS REPORT.

On reading this report, I could not forbear contrasting their mode of treating polygamy with that of the missionaries in the East, which had come under my own observation there, and which I had, at first, so severely criticised. I now began to blush at my own late ignorance and bigotry. And the more I thought of the ecclesiastical tyranny of the North-American missionaries, the higher rose my indignation against it. I could not fail to see that their narrow attachment to their own social system had made them judicially blind to the merits of any other; and that they were more ignorant of the true spirit of Christianity as well as of the natural rights of man concerning the laws of marriage, than even the poor savages themselves. Yet they undoubtedly supposed they were doing God essential service by this act of inhumanity ; just as our fathers did when they hanged and burned honest men because they worshipped God in a different manner, and entertained different views of divine truth, from themselves. Their mistake is one which has always been too common, and from which no one, perhaps, is altogether free.   It consists in assuming that because we are honest in our belief, and mean to be right, others who essentially differ from us are dishonest and wrong ; and in presuming to judge the conduct of others by what we *feel to be right*, i.e., by our own standard of morality, instead of judging them by what we *know to be right*, according to the infallible standard of divine truth.

These reflections led me to give the whole subject of marriage, in respect to its divine and natural laws, as thorough and as critical an investigation as my abilities and advantages enabled me to do ; and to inquire into the origin and the moral tendencies of the two social systems of monogamy and polygamy.

I have now pursued this investigation many years, and have become convinced that polygamy is not always an immorality ; that sometimes a man may innocently have more than one woman ; and then that it is their right to be married to him, and his duty to love and cherish them for better for worse, for richer for poorer, in sickness and in health, till death shall part them.

WHY I HAVE WRITTEN THIS BOOK.

I am unwilling to leave the world without having given it the benefit of these reflections. All truth is important. If these views are true, they ought to be known ; if they are not true let them be refuted. If the prejudices of modern Christians are opposed to the social system which their ancient brethren, the earliest saints and patriarchs, practised in the good old days of Bible truth and pastoral simplicity, I believe that these prejudices are neither natural nor inveterate ; but that they have been induced by the corrupted Christianity of the mediæval priesthood, and that they will be removed when Christian people become better informed ; and if it be necessary for me to sacrifice my own ease and my own credit, in attempting to remove them, I shall only suffer the common lot of all reformers before me. Yet I scarcely expect to see any immediate result of my labors. It is a melancholy and an humiliating fact that the opinions of most people are determined more by what others around them think and say than by what they believe themselves. They are not accustomed to the proper exercise of their own reason, and do not follow the convictions of their own minds. Yet there are some who dare to think and act for themselves; and into the hands of a few such I doubt not these pages will fall: and to all such I most heartily commend them. To an active and an ingenuous mind there is no pursuit more fascinating than the pursuit of knowledge, no pleasure more exquisite than the discovery of truth. All those who would enjoy this pleasure in its highest sense must love Truth for herself alone; they must emancipate themselves from the trammels of prejudice and public opinion, and dare to follow Truth wherever she may lead. And I make no further apology for calling the attention of an intelligent age to a new examination of an old institution. Truth dreads no scrutiny; shields herself behind no breastwork of established custom or of respectable authority, but proudly stands upon her own merits. I will not despair, therefore, of gaining the attention of every lover of the truth while I attempt to develop and demonstrate the laws of God and of nature upon the important subjects of love and marriage, and to apply those laws to the two systems of monogamy and polygamy.

THE LAWS OF GOD AND OF NATURE; THE TERMS DEFINED.

To prevent misconception of the meaning intended to be conveyed by these terms, it is proper to state, that, by the laws of God, I mean the written laws contained in the Holy Bible; which I believe to be the most perfect revelation of the divine will and God's inestimable gift to man. The laws by which the universe subsists, embracing those of mind as well as those of matter, are undoubtedly the laws of God also; but we call them, by way of distinction, the laws of nature; because it is only by a diligent study of nature, and by reasoning from cause to effect and from effect to cause, that they can be determined, yet when determined they are always found to harmonize with each other and also with the written law, which they may safely and properly be employed to illustrate and explain.

Both these classes of law differ materially from the civil law, or the laws of States and nations ; especially in these respects : the former are always harmonious with each other, and equally valid at all times and places, and are, therefore, infallible and unchangeable. The latter are always conflicting with and often contradictory to one another ; and are constantly being altered, amended, and repealed ; and, although founded upon truth, in general, and intended for the public good, and therefore entitled to our respect and obedience, they are so only in a qualified sense, far inferior to that profound respect and implicit obedience due to divine and natural law.

In my analysis of the laws of love and marriage on which depends the mutual relation of the two sexes, I shall be obliged to speak of that relation with unusual familiarity ; even though I may sometimes offend our modern notions of modesty and propriety — notions which I shall not now stop to

discuss, whether they be true or false ; it matters
not.   Truth rises superior to every consideration of
fastidiousness, and it is high time that these truths
should be demonstrated.   Yet it shall be my care
so to treat them as not to offend true modesty un-
necessarily : *puris omnia pura.*

CHAPTER II.

THE PRIMARY LAWS OF LOVE.

LOVE LIKE ELECTRICITY.

AMONG all the inherent properties of mankind, none is more important than that of love; and no one more clearly evinces the wisdom and benevolence of his Creator. Love, in its primary sense, to which it will be restricted in this treatise, is the mutual attraction of the two sexes. It exists in all persons, either as a sensibility or a passion. It is a sensibility when in a state of rest, or when exercised towards the whole of the opposite sex indiscriminately; but it is a passion when strongly excited and when exercised towards particular individuals. And it is as truly and fundamentally a law of human nature as electricity is of material nature, — to which it bears a curious analogy. We can scarcely reason with more certainty upon the laws of electricity than upon those of love, for we have the assistance of consciousness in one case which we want in the other. But note the analogy: it has been demonstrated that all bodies possess electricity in a greater or less degree; and that some are positive when compared with others, and some are negative. They are usually at rest; but when two bodies of different electrical states approach each other, they at once become highly excited, and continue so till brought in contact with each other, when the positive charges or impregnates the negative. So it is found that love exists in different states in the two sexes, and in different degrees of intensity in different individuals of the same sex. Males are positive, and females negative; and while the latter differ less from each other than the former do, being nearly all of them susceptible to the proper proposals of genuine love, yet they are not so much affected by spontaneous passion as the former are, who usually experience it with great intensity, and are impelled to make the first advances. But there are always some individuals among them who need a great deal of encouragement before they will advance and propose ; and others who are almost destitute of the common sensibility of love, and who will neither make proposals nor receive them.

LOVE REFINES AND ENNOBLES.

Love sheds on earth something of the beauty and the light of heaven. Love develops the noblest traits of humanity ; and often brings them out from those persons who had given little promise of possessing them, until they were brought under the influence of this master passion. There is nothing so great, so difficult, or so self-sacrificing that love will not inspire men to dare and to do. But it is not more in splendid achievements or wonderful adventures, than it is in the innumerable little things, which conspire to make up the happiness of social life, that the greatest victories of love are won. We cannot love any person, without seeking his or her benefit ; and in endeavoring to benefit and please the object of our affection, we are impelled to improve and beautify ourselves, in order to become more worthy of our beloved one's affection in return. And this leads us not only to adorn our persons but to polish our manners and cultivate our minds.

Hence, we are deeply indebted to this sentiment for those qualities of mind and person which combine to constitute us social beings; since it does not more certainly impel us to the acquisition of what is beautiful and becoming in dress and deportment, than to the attainment of intelligence and politeness, and to surround ourselves with all the embellishments of civilization. Love refines all that it touches. Under its influence the rough boy becomes the respectful young gentleman, and the awkward girl assumes the innate refinement of the lady. Love paints the cheek with roses, adds new lustre and intelligence to the eye, imparts strength and elasticity to the step, grace and dignity to the mien, courage to the heart, eloquence to the tongue, and poetry to every thought. In fact, love is at once the poetry of life, and the life of poetry. Love has inspired, in every age, the brightest dreams of fancy and the noblest conceptions of literature and of art, constituting the perpetual theme which animates the writer's pen and tunes the poet's lyre. Love reposes in the sculptor's marble; love blushes upon the painter's canvas. And all these various embodiments of love by literature and art are universally appreciated and admired; for the pen, the chisel, and the pencil have only given expression to the general sentiment of mankind. The poet and the artist have only wrought out what every one else had already thought: and have only given speech, form, and color to the silent, shadowy images of the common heart of man.

LOVE INHERENT TO ALL.

That the language of love is universally understood, and that its varied delineations by the inspiration of art are always and everywhere delightfully recognized, is sufficient proof that the sentiment is universally experienced. It is not confined to the gifted, the highborn, or the rich, nor is it peculiar to any period of the world, or to any condition of life. All have possessed the sensibility, if they have not experienced the passion; they have felt the want of love, if they have not enjoyed its fruition.

It is our birthright. We have no sooner passed the period of adolescence than we inherit the power and the inclination to love. We then feel an instinctive yearning of the heart for a kindred heart. We are each of us conscious of being incomplete alone, and incapable of enjoying alone our fullest happiness, and we intuitively seek that happiness by linking our destiny in life with some dear one of the opposite sex. It is there only that our natural wants can be supplied. One sex is the complement of the other. Each is imperfect alone, and each supplies what the other lacks. Self-reliant as man may suppose himself to be, yet divine wisdom has said, " It is not good for the man to be alone ; " he needs a " helpmeet " in woman. Still less is it good for the woman to be alone, for " she was created for the man," and every woman wants a man to love ; for love is her life, and it is only while she loves, or hopes to love, that she lives to any happy or useful or honest purpose. It has been said that as woman was taken out of man in her creation, so it is man's instinctive desire to seek her and to reclaim her as his own counterpart, or that portion of himself which is required to complete the symmetry of his nature and the happiness of his life. For this love the youthful heart longs and pines until it attains the object of its desires, or

3

until it has become so sordid, so hard, and so profligate, as to be, at once, unworthy of possessing it, and incapable of enjoying it. This susceptibility of the youthful heart has been faithfully portrayed by a youthful poet, in the following lines, which are at once recognized, as expressing the common sentiment of humanity : —

> " It is not that my lot is low,
>   That bids the silent tear to flow,
>   It is not grief that bids me moan,
>   It is that I am all alone.
>
>   In woods and glens I love to roam,
>   When the tired hedger hies him home ;
>   Or by the woodland pool to rest,
>   When pale the star looks on its breast.
>
>   Yet when the silent evening sighs,
>   With hallowed airs and symphonies,
>   My spirit takes another tone,
>   And sighs that it is all alone.
>
>   The woods and winds with sudden wail
>   Tell all the same unvaried tale ;
>   I've none to smile when I am free,
>   And when I sigh, to sigh with me.

> Yet in my dreams a form I view,
> That thinks on me and loves me too;
> I start! and when the vision's flown,
> I weep that I am all alone."
>
> H. K. WHITE.

Another poet has expressed the same sentiment in the following impassioned lines : —

> " Give me but
> Something whereunto I may bind my heart;
> Something to love, to cherish, and to clasp
> Affection's tendrils round."

Now, if any one should be inclined to call all this but love-sick sentimentality, unworthy our serious consideration, I shall only answer him in the words of Dr. Johnson, the English moralist: " We must not ridicule the passion of love, which he who never felt, never was happy; and he who laughs at never deserves to feel, — a passion which has inspired heroism, and subdued avarice; a passion which has caused the change of empires, and the loss of worlds."

Shall these heaven-born impulses of nature be regarded, or must they be repressed? Shall we permit these tendrils of our love to bind themselves around some kindred heart, or shall we suffer them to be rudely torn asunder, and cast aside to wither and decay? Implanted for the noblest purposes within our breasts, interwoven with the very fibres of our being, the laws of God and of nature unquestionably demand their indulgence.

LOVE IS THE RIGHT OF ALL.

In plainer terms, the laws of God and of nature clearly indicate that every man and every woman, possessing sufficient health and vitality to experience the passion of love, is benefited by its proper gratification ; and those laws both allow and invite every one to enjoy it in its full fruition. A man is not wholly a man, nor a woman wholly a woman, who has never experienced the ecstasies of gratified love. And those men and women who are spending their most vigorous period of life in cold and barren celibacy, without ever having yielded to the warm desires of reproduction, are living, every moment, in debt to their Creator and to the commonwealth of mankind. They have never fulfilled some of the most important purposes of their being.

" Torches are made to light, jewels to wear,
  Dainties to taste, fresh beauty for the use,
  Herbs for their smell, and sappy plants to bear ;
  Things growing to themselves are growth's abuse :
    Seeds spring from seeds, and beauty breedeth beauty,
    Thou wast begot — to get it is thy duty.

  Upon the earth's increase why shouldst thou feed,
  Unless the earth with thy increase be fed ?
  By law of Nature thou art bound to breed,
  That thine may live, when thou thyself art dead ;
    And so in spite of death thou dost survive,
    In that thy likeness still is left alive."

SHAKSPEARE (Venus and Adonis).

LOVE MUST BE RESTRICTED WITHIN THE LIMITS OF CHASTITY.

Yet men and women must not rush into sensual
pleasure like brutes, for we are moral beings, as
well as corporeal beings, and, as such, the subjects
of moral law, which requires us to govern our
passions, and circumscribe them within the limits
of purity. But, even in this respect, there is no
real disagreement between the laws of morality
and those of Nature : when they are properly understood, they are each equally explicit in forbidding every form of licentious impurity. The most

loathsome and incurable diseases are the penalties imposed by natural law, and the severest retributions of eternity, the penalties imposed by divine law, upon the promiscuous and unrestrained indulgence of the amorous propensity. Nor are these penalties unnecessary. No passion of our nature is more vehement, and no one more liable to be tempted and led astray from the path of rectitude; and we should, therefore, attend the more carefully to those laws and limitations which God and Nature have imposed upon its indulgence. And I cannot doubt that they have limited its indulgence strictly to the marriage relation. Some well-defined limit there must be between chastity and unchastity, and vice and virtue, or else the laws which define them and which punish transgressors must be unjust and oppressive.

MARRIAGE CONSTITUTES THAT LIMIT.

Here there is no oppression and no injustice. Everybody is born with a propensity to love, and everybody that is willing to marry may marry, and indulge that propensity in innocence and purity. Within this limit the gratification of love affords us the most exquisite pleasure, promotes health, conduces to longevity, and is entirely consistent with the rules of morality and religion. But when it oversteps this limit prescribed by our Creator, and bursts the barriers of chastity, it then assumes the form of unprincipled lust, and inflicts upon its miserable votaries the utmost torture of body, degradation of mind, and remorse of conscience.

"Marriage is honorable in all, and the bed undefiled; but whoremongers and adulterers God will judge." — Heb. xiii. 4.

"Hail wedded love, mysterious law, true source
Of human offspring, sole propriety,
In Paradise, of all things common else.
By thee adulterous lust was driven from man,
Among the bestial herd to range; by thee
Founded in reason, loyal, just, and pure
Relations dear and all the charities
Of father, son, and brother first were known.
Far be it, that I should write thee sin or blame;
Or think thee unbefitting holiest place;
Perpetual fountain of domestic sweets,
Whose bed is undefiled and chaste pronounced,
Present or past, as saints and patriarchs used.
Here Love his golden shafts employs, here lights
His constant lamp, and waves his purple wings."

PARADISE LOST, Book iv.

CHAPTER III.

PRIMARY LAWS OF MARRIAGE.

Since the infallible and unchangeable laws of God and of Nature have limited the indulgence of love to married persons only, it becomes necessary to inquire into the laws and limitations of marriage itself. What is marriage ? and who are entitled to its rights and benefits ?

MARRIAGE DEFINED.

The proper definition of marriage is the main point at issue between the social system of polygamy and that of monogamy, which it is the object of this treatise to examine and compare. One system defines marriage to be the exclusive union of one man to one woman until separated by death or divorce ; the other defines it to be the union of one man to either one woman or more, until separated, in like manner, by death or divorce.

It now remains for us to determine which of these definitions is most in harmony with the laws of God and of Nature. And we shall be better able to do this, by considering carefully the beneficent purposes which marriage is designed to subserve.

MARRIAGE BENEFICIAL.

Marriage is the first and best of all human institutions, if it can properly be called human, since it was first solemnized in Paradise, by the Creator himself, who then said, "It is not good that the man should be alone ; I will make him a help meet for him." And he made a woman, and brought her unto the man. "And God blessed them, and God said unto them, Be fruitful, and multiply, and replenish the earth, and subdue it."

It is impossible to enumerate all the benefits of marriage, since there is no vital interest of mankind which it does not affect favorably. Marriage perpetuates the human race ; lays the foundations of organized society ; promotes industry ; accumulates wealth ; cultivates the arts, and maintains religion. It builds the house, tills the soil, supports the family, and fosters every charitable and benevolent enterprise.

ALL ARE ENTITLED TO ITS BENEFITS.

As the word of God has declared marriage to be honorable in all, so we must infer that his laws have made provision for the honorable marriage of all; and that every person of each sex is equally entitled to its rights and benefits. These rights should no more be restricted to the rich and the fortunate than are the susceptibilities of love, upon which marriage properly depends, and from which it derives its only proper warrant and authority.

"Love, and love only, is the loan for love."

Marriage, when authorized and warranted by the promptings of an honest love, is a pure and blissful consummation of all that is divine in humanity; but when it is contracted from mercenary or ambitious motives, it becomes a most unholy profanation. Love was not made for marriage, but marriage for love. Love is an inherent and a necessary attribute of humanity;

marriage a subsequent relationship instituted to minister to love's wants. Love is the mistress, marriage the handmaid. Marriage must wait the demands of love, and not love the demands of marriage. It is, therefore, equally disrespectful to our Creator, and dishonorable to man, to require that love should be suppressed because marriage is inconvenient, and still more dishonorable and disrespectful to require any one to be deprived of the rights of love on account of the impossibility of marriage; for marriage ought to be possible to all. If love be refining and ennobling, if it be the spontaneous, instinctive birthright of all, and if our Creator has restricted its indulgence to the marriage relation, then marriage must be the right of all, or else God is not a benevolent being. But all nature and all revelation have demonstrated that he is a benevolent being, and it is both impious and absurd to believe that his laws have made no adequate provision for every one to be married who wishes to be. We may waive our rights, and live in celibacy, if we prefer to; but no one who *loves* and who wishes to marry ought to be compelled to remain unmarried.

It is, therefore, demonstrated that any form of society which fails to provide for the marriage of all is a defective system, and opposed to the natural, inherent, and inalienable rights of man.

THESE RIGHTS ARE DENIED TO MANY.

Yet we well know that there are very many persons, especially many women, who are neither married nor have an opportunity to marry. By some means they have been deprived of their rights. The fault is not theirs; they would, in almost every instance, prefer wedded life if it were in their power to attain it; but it is not. They possess the same susceptibilities of love, the same yearning for intimate companionship, that others do, but these tender sensibilities they are obliged to repress. The fault is not in nature, nor in the laws of God, but it is in the tyrannical laws and fashions of the artificial system of social life which now obtains among us. This system must be at fault, for it does not and it cannot provide for the marriage of all; and many who desire to marry are forever deprived of husbands and homes: while the system of polygamy does provide for all, and is, therefore, the only system which is in harmony with divine and natural laws.

This proposition is further demonstrated by the simple fact that the number of marriageable women always exceeds the number of marriageable men.

MORE WOMEN THAN MEN.

The statistics of all States and nations agree in this fact,* except, occasionally, in those States in

---

* "The censuses heretofore taken of more than one hundred millions of the population of Europe exhibit the remarkable fact, that in those countries, during the first fifteen years of life, the males uniformly exceed the females in number, but that, subsequently to this age, the females become most numerous, and increasingly so with increase of age. The same is true with regard to the proportionate numbers of the sexes in Massachusetts and the other New-England States.

"During the ten years 1856–65, the total number of births registered in Massachusetts was 334,493, of which 171,584, or 51.29 per cent, were males; 161,715, or 48.35 per cent, were females; and of 1,194, or ⅓ of one per cent, the sex was not stated. During the first ten years of life, the deaths of males exceeded those of females in a ratio beyond that of the relative number of the sexes at birth.

"In 1855, there were 32,301 more females than males in Massachusetts; in 1860, 37,640 more females; and the excess of

which the population is very largely made up by
foreign immigration. Most of these immigrants
are men ; and many of them have left their wives
and families in the mother-country, and do not
intend to become permanent citizens, but hope
to make their fortunes and return home to enjoy
them. Yet many persons who have never ex-
amined statistical tables, nor taken any other accurate means of informing themselves, suppose the
number of the men to be equal to that of the
women ; and it has been a plausible objection to
polygamy, that if some men have a plurality of
wives, some other men must thereby be deprived
of any, and the system must be unequal and unjust.
The objection would be valid were it based upon
valid facts : but it is all an error ; and it is one
which a little observation would enable almost any
one readily to correct. One has only to count up
the persons of each sex of marriageable age in all

---

females in 1865 was 63,011." — *Census of Massachusetts for* 1865,
pp. 286, 287.

"Ever since the first census of 1765, there has been found an
excess of females over males in Massachusetts; the disparity
has increased somewhat rapidly since 1850." — *Massachusetts
Registration Report of Births, Marriages, and Deaths for* 1866.
O. Warner, Secretary of Commonwealth, Boston, 1867.

the families of his own acquaintance to satisfy himself that the females will outnumber the males. It
is true, that, at birth, the number of each sex is
nearly equal; that of the males being slightly in
excess, but a much larger proportion of the males
die in childhood, than of the females.* Generally,
about fifty per cent of all male children die before
the age of twenty-one years; while only about
thirty-three per cent, or two-thirds as many females,
die during the same period.† And then, as they

---

* In Massachusetts the percentage of the deaths of male
children under one year of age during the year 1866 was 22.25,
that of female children during the same year was 17.42. See
Massachusetts Registration Report for 1866, p. 44.

† STATISTICAL TABLES.

POP. OF MASSACHUSETTS, June 1, A.D. 1860.

			Male.	Female.
Under 1 year,			15,869	15,666
1 and under 5,			60,059	59,695
5	"	10,	64,476	64,050
10	"	15,	57,544	56,804
15	"	20,	57,070	63,730
20	"	30,	112,413	132,106
Total,			596,713	634,353

COLORED POP. N.Y. CITY, 1860.

			Male.	Female.
Under 1 year,			82	114
1 and under 5,			410	453
5	"	10,	566	574
10	"	15,	565	531
15	"	20,	446	648
20	"	30,	1,120	1,655
Total,			5,468	7,106

WHITE POP. OF SUFFOLK CO., (City of Boston), Mass., 1860.

			Male.	Female.
Under 1 year,			2,707	2,743
1 and under 5,			9,358	9,334
5	"	10,	9,730	9,945
10	"	15,	8,224	8,313
15	"	20,	19,865	23,906
Total,			91,015	99,234

POP. OF PENNSYLVANIA, 1860.

			Male.	Female.
Under 1 year,			44,167	42,704
1 and under 5,			179,253	176,115
5	"	10,	194,258	191,094
10	"	15,	171.162	167,025
15	"	20,	149,531	160,357
20	"	30,	246,343	263,931
Total,			1,454,419	1,451,796

grow up to manhood, the boys and young men are constantly exposed to hardships and dangers, from which the softer sex is exempt; and hence the excess of the females goes on continually increasing, as we see by the statistical tables, from the beginning to the end of the marriageable age. All this in times of peace: the excess must be much greater than usual after a destructive war; for during the late civil war in America there were lost from both parties nearly a million of men in the most productive period of life.

POP. OF N. YORK STATE, 1860.			POP. OF PHIL. CO., PENN., (White), 1860.		
	Male.	Female.		Male.	Female.
Under 1 year,	52,175	51,257	Under 1 year,	7,829	7,475
1 and under 5,	216,112	210,591	1 and under 5,	30,864	30,533
5 " 10,	232,426	227,413	5 " 10,	31,981	31,737
10 " 15,	203,453	197,884	10 " 15,	26,135	27,113
15 " 20,	188,893	205,604	15 " 20,	23,425	29,204
20 " 30,	341,037	386,141	20 " 30,	49,667	61,380
Total,	1,933,532	1,947,203	Total,	260,156	283,188

WHITE POP. OF N.Y.CITY, 1860.			POP. OF PHILADELPHIA. (Colored), 1860.		
	Male.	Female.		Male.	Female.
Under 1 year,	12,247	12,072	Under 1 year,	187	209
1 and under 5,	47,074	46,025	1 and under 5,	809	1,065
5 " 10,	46,380	45,452	5 " 10,	1,019	1,195
10 " 15,	36,233	34,936	10 " 15,	996	1,199
15 " 20,	33,344	39,628	15 " 20,	915	1,45?
20 " 30,	77,747	97,627	20 " 30,	1,875	2,864
Total,	391,521	409,567	Total,	9,177	13,008

The foregoing statistics are compiled from the United-States Census for 1860. The following are from the Census of Massa-

WOMEN MATURE EARLIER THAN MEN.

Young women become marriageable at a much earlier age than young men do. There is a natural or constitutional difference of several years, and prudential considerations cause the difference to become practically greater. But few young men are born to large fortunes, which these times of extravagance require for the fashionable maintenance of a family; and those who are rich are not always the most prompt to marry. They prefer to spend their early manhood in dissipation, and are unwilling to bow to the yoke of wedlock till

---

chusetts for 1865, published under the supervision of O. Warner, Secretary of the Commonwealth. Table I. p. 2.

POP. OF MASSACHUSETTS, June 1, 1865.			POP. OF SUFFOLK CO., MASS. (City of Boston), June 1, 1865.			
	Male.	*Female.*	Under 1 year,		2,145	2,017
Under 1 year,	11,974	11,745	1 and under 2,		2,003	1,819
1 and under 2,	12,898	12,431	2 " 3,		2,288	2,255
2 " 3,	13,643	13,515	3 " 4,		2,205	2,233
3 " 4,	14,161	14,188	4 " 5,		2,280	2,301
4 " 5,	14,735	14,653	5 " 10,		11,267	11,623
5 " 10,	71,777	71,614	10 " 15,		9,848	9,971
10 " 15,	63,853	62,838	15 " 20,		8,527	10,267
15 " 20,	55,281	61,890	20 " 30,		17,601	25,618
20 " 30,	96,027	129,479				
			Total,		96,529	111,683
Total,	602,010	665,021				

In the above table the excess of females between the ages of 15 and 20 is 6,609, or about $\frac{1}{8}$ of the number of males; between 20 and 30 it is 33,452, or more than $\frac{1}{3}$ of the number of males.

4

they begin to feel the infirmities of age; while the poor man must devote several years of his majority to toil before he becomes able to assume matrimonial expenses. The result is that most men do not marry until between twenty-five and thirty-five years of age, and many at a later period; while a large majority of women who marry at all are married between the ages of fifteen and twenty-five. On the whole, therefore, women are practically marriageable ten years younger than men are, a period which constitutes a third part of the average duration of adult life. From these two causes alone, — the greater number of women, and their being marriageable so much younger, — the proportion of marriageable women to marriageable men would be about two to one.

MANY MEN REFUSE TO MARRY.

But the practical difference is still greater. For after men have arrived at adult manhood, and have acquired the means of supporting a family, many of them refuse marriage. Some have outlived their youthful desires, and have acquired decided habits of celibacy; some are too gay and too profligate ; others too busy and too selfish ; others so broken down by early dissipation and diseased by the contagious poison of low vice, that they are totally unfit to marry : while there are many others whose occupations (such as sailors and soldiers) most commonly prevent marriage. From these disabilities the other sex is much more exempt. They are exposed to fewer temptations ; they are more susceptible to religious impressions ; they are more immediately under the control of parents and guardians, and are saved from many of those enervating and degrading habits which beset young men, rendering them either disinclined to marriage, or unfit for it, or both.

FEW WOMEN DECLINE MARRIAGE.

There are, on the other hand, few women who are unwilling to marry. They are naturally dependent upon their male friends ; and, after the period of childhood, this dependence is seldom happy or even tolerable, except in the marriage relation. The former is a dependence of necessity, the latter is, or ought to be, a dependence of love ; and this distinction makes all the difference in the world.

Hence it needs no argument to prove what is so
universally admitted, that women fulfil their highest destiny in life only by becoming wives and
mothers. I will cite a woman's testimony, and
submit the case, quoting the earnest words of
" GAIL HAMILTON." " There is not one woman
in a million who would not be married if . . . she
could have a chance. How do I know? Just as
I know that the stars are now shining in the sky,
though it is high noon. I never saw a star at
noonday ; but I know it is the nature of stars to
shine in the sky, and of the sky to hold its stars.
Genius or fool, rich or poor, beauty or the beast,
if marriage were what it should be, what God
meant it to be, what even, with the world's present
possibilities, it might be, it would be the Elysium,
the sole, complete Elysium, of woman, yes, and of
man. Greatness, glory, usefulness, happiness,
await her otherwheres ; but here alone all her
powers, all her being, can find full play. No condition, no character even, can quite hide the gleam
of the sacred fire ; but on the household hearth it
joins the warmth of earth to the hues of heaven.
Brilliant, dazzling, vivid, a beacon and a blessing

her light may be ; but only a happy home blends the prismatic rays into a soft, serene whiteness, that floods the world with divine illumination. Without wifely and motherly love, a part of her nature must remain enclosed, a spring shut up, a fountain sealed." *

MONOGAMY PREVENTS MARRIAGE.

But under the system of monogamy it is impossible for half the women to live in the enjoyment of the married state. This cruel and oppressive system is compelling them either to repress the fondest sensibilities and the most imperative demands of Nature, and to renounce their dearest rights, or else to assert them in a clandestine and forbidden manner, and thus to abandon themselves to a life of infamy and an eternity of shame and woe.

In older and more wealthy countries practising monogamy, the comparative number of unmarried to married women is even greater. The statistical tables of England show that less than one-third of the marriageable women of that country were living in marriage at the time of the last census.

* New Atmosphere, p. 55.

At the period of the highest glory of the Roman empire, and also during its long decline, while wealth and luxury increased, and the artificial conventionalities of society were greatly multiplied, it was observed, with alarm, that marriages became less and less frequent, and were consummated later and later in life : and all the power of the government was exerted in vain to arrest the growing evil. Heavy fines and special taxes were levied upon old bachelors, and high premiums paid to persons having numerous families ; but the evil continued to increase till the empire was dismembered.*

---

* " But neither rewards nor penalties proved effectual to check the increasing tendency to celibacy; and at the period of the Gracchi an alarm was sounded that the old Roman race was becoming rapidly extinguished. . . . When the legislation of Julius Cæsar was found ineffectual for controlling the still growing evil, it was re-enforced by his successor with fresh penalties and rewards." — *Merivale's Hist. of the Romans,* chap. 33, vol. 2, pp. 37, 38.

" But upon this one point the master of the Romans [Augustus] could make no impression upon the dogged disobedience of his subjects: both the men and the women preferred the loose terms of union upon which they had consented to cohabit, &c." — *Ibid.*

" Augustus most anxiously, both by law and precept, en-

THE MARRIAGE CEREMONY.

In respect to the mode of performing the marriage ceremony, the divine law does not prescribe
any : and nothing more was necessary, in ancient
times, to constitute a valid marriage than a mutual
agreement, or actual cohabitation. The ancient Romans had three different modes of tying the hyme-
neal knot, each with a different degree of looseness,
but none of them so firm as it should be. The
ceremony has always varied in different States, and
at different times in the same State, and should
never be regarded as any thing more than a public
recognition of a relationship already formed and
completed between the parties. Yet as marriage

---

couraged marriage; but the profligacy of the manners which
then prevailed was such that all the honors and rewards and
immunities which he prepared were of but little avail." —
Keightley's Hist. of the Roman Empire, chap i., p. 11.

"The principal cause of the prevalent aversion to marriage
was the extreme dissoluteness of manners at that time, exceed-
ing any thing known in modern days. . . . The first law on the
subject was the Julian '*De Maritandis Ordinibus*,' of 736; and
this having proved ineffectual, a new and more comprehensive
law, embracing all the provisions of the Julian, and named the
'*Papia-Poppœan*,' was passed in the year 762." — *Ibid.*, chap. 2,
p. 34.

is a matter of important consequence to the friends and kindred of the parties, and also to the whole State, involving public as well as private obligations, it is eminently proper that some appropriate ceremony should be performed, and that it should be sufficiently public to leave no doubt as to its reality. Yet marriages are made in heaven; the claim of the Romish Church to make and unmake them is a blasphemous assumption. No ceremony can add to their religious validity; and it can only be necessary to their legality and publicity.

CHAPTER IV.

ORIGIN OF POLYGAMY.

PREJUDICES TO BE OVERCOME.

HAVING thus fulfilled my promise to analyze and demonstrate the fundamental laws of love and marriage, I shall now attempt, with equal candor and simplicity, to trace the origin and indicate the moral characteristics of the two social systems of monogamy and polygamy, and to apply to them the same tests of philosophical analysis and comparison. And here allow me again to say that it is necessary to arm ourselves with patient candor, or we cannot appreciate the truth and justice of any fair analysis of these systems. As we have been brought up under the system of monogamy, we have inherited the prejudices of that system; and, having been taught to look upon the opposite one with detestation and contempt, we are, on that account, but ill cualified to judge between them.

Let us remember that, whether our prejudices are right or wrong, they are prejudices only. We have not stopped to reason; we have been content to cherish our opinions on this subject without examination and without reason. We have always accustomed ourselves to believe that polygamy originated in barbarism; that it is perpetuated by barbarians only, and that it panders to the basest and most depraved of human passions. But let us now think for ourselves. For one, I claim that right. I dare to question the superior purity of monogamy; and on behalf of the despised and persecuted system of polygamy, I venture to appeal from the rash decisions of prejudice to the solemn tribunals of divine and natural law; and in support of this appeal I cite the facts of sacred and profane history, and plead the inalienable rights of man.

POLYGAMY IS NOT BARBARISM.

If European monogamists have hitherto surpassed all other men in civilization and social happiness, it is not on account of their **monogamy**, but, no doubt, on account of their Christianity. Even a perverted Christianity, a corrupted Chris-

tianity, a Roman Christianity, is better than idolatry or Mohammedanism. What, then, may we not
hope when Christianity shall become free and
pure, and restored to its pristine simplicity and
glory?

An idolatrous nation practising monogamy has
never been able long to exist. History does not
furnish one example. Such nations soon become
so incurably corrupt as to incur the wrath of God,
and are swept from the face of the earth. Neither
civilization nor barbarism; military power or pusil-
lanimity; tyranny or freedom; monarchy, aristoc-
racy, or democracy; literature, art, wealth, genius,
or stupidity has ever been able to save them. Many
such States and nations have started in the race of
glory and perpetual empire; but each of them has
come to premature decay. Such were the different
States of ancient Greece and ancient Italy, many
of them distinguished for having produced men of
the most brilliant genius and the most renowned experience in the various arts of peace and war, and
several of them achieving extensive conquests and
becoming vast empires; yet they very soon collapsed
and went to ruin. And such was the fate of the

many scores or perhaps hundreds of the petty States of all Europe before the establishment of Christianity. They rose, they flourished, they became licentious, they fell. Wave after wave of the purer races of the polygamists of Asia rolled over them, and assumed their places ; and as these, in turn, fell into their social habits, and adopted their monogamy, and became corrupt, they also became extinct, and were succeeded by newer and purer immigrations. On the other hand, the polygamists of Asia have preserved their social purity, and along with it many of their nationalities, through every age, notwithstanding their idolatry and Mohammedanism. Such are the nations of China, Japan, Persia, and Arabia, whose living languages and existing laws date back to the very earliest records of antiquity. An intelligent Christian nation practising polygamy has never yet existed, simply because the two institutions have hitherto been falsely deemed incompatible and irreconcilable. The Gnostic heresy had so soon corrupted the springs of Christian learning, and the Grecian and Roman hierarchies had so soon usurped the seats of Christian authority, that the freedom and simplicity of the pristine faith were perverted, even before such an experiment could be made, as I shall fully demonstrate in the next chapter ; and now it is most probable that if such an experiment shall ever be made, it will be somewhere upon the continent of free America.

> " Westward the course of empire takes its way ;
> The four first acts already past,
> A fifth shall close the drama with the day, —
> Time's noblest offspring is the last."

Polygamy is not barbarism, for it has been maintained and supported by such men as Abraham, Moses, David, and Solomon ; whose superiors in all that constitute the highest civilization — knowledge, piety, wisdom, and refinement of mind and manners — the world has never known, either in ancient or modern times. Yet polygamy, though it be not barbarism, has almost always and everywhere prevailed, where a simple, natural, and inartificial state of society subsists. Its origin is coeval with that of the human race. It is mentioned before the flood. It is mentioned soon after the flood. As soon as mankind were multiplied upon the earth, it was discovered that the number of the women exceeded that of the men ; and also that the amorous passions of the men were stronger than those of the women.   Polygamy brings both these inequalities together, and allows them to correct each other.   It furnishes every woman who wishes to marry, a husband and a home ; and gives every man an opportunity of expending his superabundant vitality in an honest way.

WHY GOD MADE BUT ONE WOMAN.

If it be objected that God created but one woman for Adam, it is a sufficient answer to reply, that both the man and the woman were also created perfect.   They were perfect in health, and perfect in morals.   But we are now imperfect in both respects ; and we now need a social system adapted to men and women as they are.   If humanity shall ever be restored to its pristine strength and beauty, the equality of the sexes will also be restored, and there will be a man for every woman, and a woman for every man ; a true woman without imperfection, whose accomplishments will not be superficial, nor whose attractions artificial ; but whose rosy cheeks and pearly teeth and swelling breasts and clustering ringlets shall be all her own. God speed the day ! Should I live to see it, I would become an advocate for monogamy. But, as it now is, there is not a man for every woman ; and either some women must remain unmarried and " waste their sweetness on the desert air," and be entirely deprived of their birthright, and denied all matrimonial advantages, or they may, several of them, agree to share those advantages in common with each other, by having a single husband between them. Polygamy does not compel them to do this : it only permits them to do it in case they have no opportunity to do better. On the other hand, it does not compel a man to marry even one woman, much less to have more ; but, if the intensity of his passion urges him to such lengths that he must have and will have more than one, it requires him to take them honestly and honorably, and to support them and be a true husband to them.

POLYGAMY TAUGHT IN THE BIBLE.

The Sacred Scriptures represent the wisest and best men that ever lived, as practising polygamy with the divine blessing and approval. David had

seven wives before he reigned in Jerusalem, " and
he took more concubines and wives out of Jerusalem, after he was come from Hebron," for God
" gave him the house of Saul and the wives of
Saul into his bosom." *   When God reproved
Abimelech, king of Gerar, for his intended adultery
with Sarah, wife of Abraham, he did, at the same
time, approve of his polygamy ; for Abimelech
said, " In the integrity of my heart and innocency
of my hands have I done this." " Said he not
unto me, She is my sister ? and she, even she
herself, said, He is my brother." And God said,
" I know that thou didst this in the integrity of
thy heart : " " now, therefore, restore the man his
wife." " And God healed Abimelech and his wife
and his maid-servants." God could allow him to
live in open polygamy, without reproof, and " in
the integrity. of his heart," but could not allow
him to commit adultery, even ignorantly.†   Solomon was reproved for multiplying the number of
his wives to an unreasonable and ostentatious degree, but more especially for having taken them

---

* 2 Sam. iii. 2-5, 14; v. 13; xii. 8. ·   † Gen. xx.

from heathen nations; for " they turned away his heart after other gods : " but these are the only reasons assigned for his reproof, there being no intimation that polygamy was wrong in itself. But it is unnecessary to cite other examples from the Bible. No one familiar with that book has ever denied that polygamy is taught in the Old Testament, and yet most Christians suppose it to be forbidden in the New. Have we any right to such a supposition? Are we right in entertaining *any supposition* on this subject? If it is forbidden in the New Testament, have we not a right to demand the most unequivocal and undoubted proofs of such prohibition? Is the God of Abraham and Isaac and Jacob the Christian's God, or is he not? Is it not possible that this supposition is an error? And, if it be an error, is it not possible that it has been one means of lessening our reverence for the Old Testament, and thereby undermining our confidence in the Bible as a whole? If this supposition be an error, has it not been tending to make infidels of us all? I copy the following paragraph from an essay of the Rev. S. W. Foljambe, recently delivered by him, at a Sabbath-

5

school Teachers' Convention at Boston, with my most hearty commendation : —

"It is sad to believe that infidelity in some form prevails throughout our State, yet we cannot doubt that it is even so, generally covert with an outward profession of regard for Christianity, but nevertheless real, accompanied by a disregard and disbelief of the scriptures of the Old and New Testaments. I refer to this not as any proof that Protestantism or Christianity is or can be a failure, or that the Scriptures are in any real danger, but as indicating a responsibility resting on us to maintain and defend the equal authority and inspiration of the Holy Scriptures; that "all scripture is given by inspiration of God;" that its writers, whether Moses or David, Isaiah or Paul, Ezekiel or John, were 'holy men of God who wrote as they were moved by the Holy Ghost.' Is it not true, that, among many who hold to the truth and reality of a divine revelation, there has come to be a feeling that in some way the New Testament has superseded the Old, and that the Old has ceased to be 'profitable for doctrine, for correction, for reproof, for instruction in righteousness'? Now, if this can be demonstrated, what is there to prove that in a still more advanced stage of spiritual life, as is claimed by many, the New Testament itself may not be superseded by some wiser interpretations of the meaning and purpose of Christ's life, and the Gospels of Matthew and of John be superseded by the gospel of Strauss or Renan; or the interpretations of Paul as to the person and work of Christ be superseded by the interpretation of Parker and of Music Hall?

"It seems to me that our Lord is explicit on this point, that the Jewish Scriptures were not and could not be superseded by any later revelation even by himself: 'Think not that I am come to destroy the law, or the prophets: I am not come to destroy, but to fulfil;' and again — 'Had ye believed Moses, ye would have believed me, for he wrote of me;' and he is continually quoting them as authority, showing that there is no inconsistency between the two revelations. Together they form one continuous and connected divine word. True, the Scriptures are composed of books that are cumulative and progressive, but they are interdependent. The internal meaning of the two parts is entirely harmonious. The divine Spirit is in them both. They never contradict, but always interpret, explain, and illustrate each other."

But let the inspiration and perpetual authority of the Old Testament be fully admitted, yet the modern Christian may say, " We do not live under the First Covenant, nor observe the ceremonies of Moses ; but we live in the New Dispensation, under the full light of the gospel : Christ has fulfilled the ritual and emblematical ordinances of the law, and set them aside ; and it is presumed that the ancient marriage laws have been set aside among the rest, and superseded by the purer system of monogamy." But this assumption cannot be supported either by sufficient testimony or by valid reasoning. The social system of polygamy had existed before the time of Moses, and had no dependence upon the ceremonial law which was instituted in his day. That law only confirmed it as a pre-existent institution. Marriage laws cannot be regarded as merely ritual and emblematical : they are moral and fundamental, guarding the dearest rights and punishing the deepest wrongs of mankind. They are, therefore, equally permanent with those laws

protecting life and property, those inculcating obedience to parents and rulers, and those maintaining
the sanctity of oaths. All these, together with the
marriage laws, existed before the time of Moses,
and have survived the time of Christ. They are
among those "laws" that Jesus came not to *subvert*
but to *ratify;* as Dr. George Campbell of Edin-
burgh has, in Matt. v. 17, very exactly translated
the terms καταλῦσαι and πληρῶσαι. Hence the marriage system of polygamy never formed a part of
that ceremonial dispensation which was abrogated
by the New Testament; nor has it ever been proved
that the New Testament was designed to affect any
change in it; but the presumption is that this new
dispensation has also left it, as it found it, — abid-
ing still in force. If any change were to be made
in an institution of such long standing, confirmed
by positive law, it could obviously be made only by
equally positive and explicit ordinances or enactments of the gospel. But such enactments are
wanting. Christ himself was altogether silent in
respect to polygamy, not once alluding to it; yet
it was practised at the time of his advent throughout Judæa and Galilee, and in all the other countries

of Asia and Africa, and, without doubt, by some
of his own disciples.

The Book of the Acts is equally silent as the four
Gospels are.   No allusion to it is found in any of
the sermons or instructions or discussions of the
apostles and early saints recorded in that book.   It
was not because Jesus or the apostles durst not
condemn it, had they considered it sinful, that they
did not speak of it, for Jesus hesitated not to denounce the sins of hypocrisy, covetousness, and
adultery, and even to alter and amend, apparently,
the ancient laws respecting divorce and retaliation ;
but he never rebuked them for their polygamy, nor
instituted any change in that system.   And this
uniform silence, so far as it implies any thing, implies approval.   John the Baptist was thrown into
prison, where he was afterwards beheaded, for reproving King Herod on account of his adultery :
and we cannot doubt, that, if he had considered
polygamy to be sinful, he would have mentioned it ;
for Herod's father was, just before that time, living with nine wives, whose names are recorded by
Josephus, in his " Antiquities of the Jews ; " *

---

* Antiq. Jud., book 17, chap. 1, § 3.

but John only reproved him for marrying Herodias, his brother Philip's wife, while his brother was living. He administered the same reproof to Herod that Nathan had formerly done to David, and for similar reasons. The apostles always denounced the sins of fornication and adultery, but never denounced polygamy, nor intimated in any way that it was a sin. In all the long and painful catalogues of sins enumerated in the first, second, and third chapters of Romans, many of which relate to the unlawful indulgence of the amorous propensities, polygamy is not once named. It is the very place where it is morally certain that it would have been named if it were sinful; and, that it is not there named, we are fully warranted to believe that it is not sinful.

MONOGAMY OF BISHOPS AND DEACONS.

The only portions of the Sacred Writings which seem to disapprove of polygamy are found in the epistles of Paul concerning the qualifications of bishops and deacons. These passages have been variously interpreted by various commentators. Some suppose that it forbids

these officers of the church from contracting a
second marriage after the death of the first wife;
others that it forbids any but married persons
being inducted into these sacred offices — that
they must be the husbands of one wife, at least,
— but that it does not forbid them taking more.
But the commonly received opinion, and the one
to which I am myself inclined, is, that in choos-
ing men for these offices, such men should be
chosen who are not much inclined to amorous
pleasures, and each of whom has one wife only.
They should be men of peculiar temperance and
sobriety.   This implies that polygamy was still
practised in the primitive Christian churches;
for otherwise it would have been superfluous and
irrelevant to mention this as a special qualification
in a candidate for one of those offices.   And
even this recommendation applies only to candidates, and not to those who have been already
ordained.   In confirmation of these views I here
cite the authority of James McKnight, D.D., one
of the most learned commentators on the New
Testament.

"As the Asiatic nations universally practised

polygamy, from an inordinate love of the pleasures of the flesh, the apostle ordered, by inspiration, that none should be made bishops but those, who, by avoiding polygamy, had showed themselves temperate in the use of sensual pleasures. . . . It may be objected, perhaps, that the gospel ought to have prohibited the people, as well as the ministers of religion, from polygamy and divorce, if these things were morally evil. As to divorce, the answer is, all, both clergy and people, were restrained from unjust divorces by the precept of Christ. With respect to polygamy being an offence against political prudence, rather than against morality, it had been permitted to the Jews by Moses, and was generally practised by the Eastern nations as a matter of indifferency; it was, therefore, to be corrected mildly and gradually, by example rather than by express precept, without occasioning those domestic troubles and causeless divorces which must necessarily have ensued, if, by an express injunction of the apostles, husbands, immediately on their becoming Christians, had been obliged to put away all their wives except one." — *Commentary on* 1 *Tim.* iii. 2.

This testimony is specially valuable as being extorted, by the force of truth, from an avowed advocate of monogamy. Although it is highly colored by that system, yet these *four points* are distinctly admitted. 1. That polygamy was commonly practised by the primitive Christians. 2. That it had been expressly permitted in the Old Testament. 3. That it was not prohibited in the New Testament. 4. That it was from political and prudential considerations, and not from any immorality in it, that candidates for the ministry were recommended to abstain from it. Hence, we conclude that this recommendation of the apostle was made out of respect to the prejudices of the Greeks and Romans, under whose laws they were then living, and who practised a corrupt and licentious monogamy, which I shall describe in the next chapter. It was doubtless for similar reasons that the same apostle recommended to the Corinthian Christians not to marry; but no one except a Shaking Quaker or a Roman Catholic can believe that such a recommendation was intended to apply to all persons, at all times and places, or that it was proper then, on any

other ground than the notorious corruption of
Corinthian morals. See Appendix, page 253.

Now polygamy is either right, or it is wrong. If
it is wrong, it is contrary to the will of God. If
it is contrary to the will of God now, it always has
been, ever since the fall of man; for God has not
changed, human nature has not changed, and the
mutual relation of the sexes has not changed. If
it is contrary to the divine will, God would certainly have expressed decided disapprobation of it
in his word, and denounced those who practised
it. But on the contrary, it was, by the Mosaic
law, expressly sanctioned, and, under certain circumstances, expressly commanded, as fully appears
from Deut. xxii. 28, and xxv. 5. In the former
passage it was commanded that if any man
(whether married or unmarried) had had illicit
intercourse with an unbetrothed virgin, then he
must marry her, and must not put her away all
his life. In the other passage it was commanded
that when a married man died without issue, his
brother *must marry* his widow. And this command is positive, whether the surviving brother
have a wife already, or not; and even if several

such married brothers should die, and leave no offspring, the surviving brother would be obliged, by this law, to marry all the widows; and in each case, the first-born children would succeed to the inheritances of their mothers' first husbands, but the younger children would belong to their own father. This was a law in Israel long before the ceremonial law of Moses, as we learn from the 38th chapter of Genesis, where it is stated that Onan the son of Judah was required to marry the widow of his brother Er, and because he took a wicked course to prevent having offspring by her, he was put to death by the immediate act of God. The entire Book of Ruth, also, constitutes a beautiful illustration and commentary of this ancient law; and it is mentioned in the New Testament in such terms as to imply that it was still in force in the time of Christ (Matt. xxii. 24–28).

POLYGAMY APPROVED OF GOD.

I sum up the divine testimony thus: If polygamy is now a vice and a sin, like adultery or lying or stealing, it always has been and always

will be a sin; and God would never have ap-
proved or commanded it: but we have seen above,
that he has commanded it in two cases at least,
viz., in case of the married man's illicit intercourse with an unbetrothed virgin, and in case of
the married man's brother's widow; and in these
cases, therefore, it cannot be a sin. In further
proof of its innocence, let it be remembered that
it was practised without rebuke by Abraham,
when he was styled "The Friend of God;" by
Jacob, when his name was changed to Israel on
account of his piety and his faith; by David,
when God himself "gave testimony, and said, I
have found David the son of Jesse a man after
my own heart;" and by many others whose
names will be held in everlasting remembrance,
being preserved in Holy Writ, long after those of
modern pseudo-religionists, who now denounce
polygamy as barbarous and sinful, shall have
perished in oblivion.

CHAPTER V.

ORIGIN OF MONOGAMY.

MONOGAMY IS THE DISSOLUTE DAUGHTER OF PA-
GANISM AND ROMANISM.

I HAVE demonstrated that monogamy is not commanded in the Bible, and that it is not the doctrine
of Christianity. I shall now account for its origin,
by proving that it is the joint offspring of paganism
and Romanism. The social system of European
monogamy is proved to be derived from the ancient
Greeks and Romans (especially from the latter),
by the early histories of the nations of Europe, and
by an uninterrupted descent of traditional customs
from them to our own times. It is one of those
pagan abominations which we have inherited, which
the Roman Church has sanctioned and confirmed,
and from which we find it so difficult to emancipate
ourselves.

IMPURITY OF ANCIENT GREEK AND ROMAN MORALS.

The ancient Greek and Roman notions of marriage and of chastity were in some respects different from ours, but only as Christianity has made them different. We are ready to admit, at least in theory, what Christianity requires, that the laws of chastity are binding upon men and women equally, and that no person can innocently indulge in amorous pleasure except with his own wife or her own husband. But among them this rule of chastity applied to the female sex alone. The other sex claimed and exercised their freedom from it, without concealment or palliation, and at the same time without the loss of moral character or of public estimation. To be grossly addicted to whoredom and seduction was no dishonor: it was only when convicted of Sodomy that they were pronounced unchaste.

Marriage was not expected or intended to preserve the public purity, or to secure domestic happiness, but was rather designed to perpetuate their heroic races, to preserve their rich patrimonial estates, and to maintain the ascendency of their

aristocratic families. For these purposes they
guarded the chastity of their wives with vigilant
jealousy and punished their adultery with severity ;
but the men placed themselves under no such restrictions either in law or in fact, but they habitu-
ally sought their own pleasures away from home,
in the public haunts of impurity, at the house of an
Aspasia, of a Leona, or of a Messalina, or at some
other establishment of their numerous Cyprian and
Corinthian dames ; or, if they could not pay the
extravagant prices demanded by these celebrated
beauties, they could at least resort to their public
temples, and gratify their lust among the prostitutes
kept there.*

---

* " The Greeks had but little pleasure in the society of their
wives. At first, the young husband only visited her by stealth :
to be seen in company with her was a disgrace." — *Bulwer's
Hist. of Athens*, book i. chap. 6.

"In the times of Corinthian opulence and prosperity, it is
said that the shrine of Venus was attended by no less than one
thousand female slaves dedicated to her service as courtesans.
These priestesses of Venus contributed not a little to the wealth
and luxury of the city." — *Anthon's Classical Dict., art. "Co-
rinthus."*

Strabo, in his great work on Geography, in speaking of the

THEIR MARRIAGES NOT PERMANENT.

The monogamy of the ancient Romans, from and after the time of two hundred years at least before the Christian era, did not require their marriages to be permanent. The principle of a life-long relationship between the husband and wife, which both Moses and Christ have insisted upon, formed no part of their social system. Marriage, among them, was not so much a religious ceremony inculcating and requiring solemn vows of binding obligation, as a civil compact, instituted for purposes of mere present convenience or family aggrandizement. It originated in policy rather than in love. They were not, of course, destitute of the passion

---

temple of Venus in Corinth says, " There were more than a thousand harlots, the slaves of the temple, who, in honor of the goddess, prostituted themselves to all comers for hire; and through these the city was crowded, and became wealthy." — Book 8, p. 151.

" Gravely impressing upon his wife and daughters that to sing and dance, to cultivate the knowledge of languages, to exercise the taste and understanding, was the business of the hired courtesan, it was to the courtesan that he repaired himself for the solace of his own lighter hours." — *Merivale's Hist. of the Romans*, vol. ii., chap. 33, p. 32.   D. Appleton & Co., 1864.

6

of love, for they were human beings; but that passion was permitted to influence them but little in contracting their marriages. They systematically degraded their love into lust. Their monogamy required it. Whenever they loved a woman they would manage to enjoy her favors without marriage. Seduction, adultery, and whoredom were rather the rule than the exception among them; but marriage was for other and more important purposes than those of love. It was rather an alliance of interests than of affections, and an affinity of families rather than of hearts.

And as policy made marriages, so policy often unmade them. If a man could, at any time, form a new alliance which would give him more wealth or influence, he always felt himself at liberty to divorce his wife, and form that new alliance. It was not uncommon, among them, for a man to have had half a dozen different wives, in, perhaps, as many years.

CONSEQUENCES OF THEIR FREQUENT DIVORCES.

Imbecility and barrenness, the usual penalties which Nature inflicts upon the violators of the marriage laws, came upon them. Their children were few and short lived, and in order to maintain their family influence, and transmit their names and their wealth to future generations, which it was their great ambition to do, they were obliged to resort to the expedient of very frequent adoptions, by taking the children of distant relations, or of those allied to them by marriage, and calling them their own. And such were the frequency of their divorces, and the intricacy of their relationships caused by their numerous adoptions, that it has been almost impossible for the best historians and biographers to give us any intelligible account of their families. Such authors as Gibbon, Anthon, Keightley, and Merivale, who are usually accurate in other respects, are found utterly at fault, when they undertake to state the relationship which the most eminent personages of Roman history bear to one another.*

---

* *Contradictions and Inaccuracies of Eminent Historians.*

ANTHON. — In art. " Drusus," in his Classical Dictionary, Dr. Charles Anthon says that Drusus " was born three months after his mother's marriage with Augustus; " but in art. " Livia " he says, " She had already borne two sons to her first husband, viz., Tiberius and Drusus, and was six months gone in pregnancy

THE MONOGAMY OF THE CÆSARS.

In order to give some just conception of Roman monogamy at that time when it first came in

---

with another child, which was the only one she ever had after her union with Augustus, and which died almost at the moment of its birth."

In art. "Julia II.," he calls her the mother of Augustus; and in art. "Augustus," he says his mother was Atia, the daughter of Julia.

In art. "Julia IV.," he calls Scribonia the first wife of Augustus; but in art. "Augustus," he calls her his third wife.

In art. "Messalina," he says she was the first wife of Claudius; and in art. "Ælia Pætina," he says Ælia was the former wife of Claudius, and that she was repudiated to make way for Messalina. And, according to Suetonius, Ælia was, in fact, the fourth, and Messalina the fifth, of his wives.

In art. "Julius Cæsar," he says his first wife was divorced in consequence of the affair of Clodius; but in art. "Clodius," he says it was against Pompeia that Clodius had illicit designs, and in art. "Pompeia," he says she was Cæsar's third wife, &c.

KEIGHTLEY.— In his Hist. of Rom. Empire, p. 11, he says, Scribonia was the first wife of Augustus; but she was his third. On the same page he says Tiberius married Agrippina, who was the younger daughter of Agrippa: but Tiberius did not marry her, but he married Vipsania, her older sister; and his brother Drusus married Agrippina, and he was the only husband she ever had, which was a remarkable circumstance for Roman ladies in those days.

On the same page he repeats the error of Anthon mentioned

contact with Christianity, and when it began to impose its social system upon the other nations of

---

above, — that Drusus was born after his mother's marriage with Augustus. Two similar errors occur on p. 13.

LIDDELL. — On p. 726 of Dr. Liddell's Hist. of Rome, there are three errors of this kind within the limits of twice as many lines, viz., he calls the name of one of Augustus's wives Clodia for Claudia; he says Scribonia was his second wife, for his third; and says that Livia, at the time of her marriage to Augustus, was pregnant of her second child instead of her third. Thus it is demonstrated that very respectable modern historians are accustomed to perpetuate error by compiling and copying from each other, when they should, every one of them, go back to the original and exact authorities, and thus eliminate the truth.

Messrs. Harper & Brothers, New York, have republished the above work of Dr. Liddell, so faithfully as to give us page for page, line for line, and word for word, an exact reprint of the English edition by John Murray; reproducing not only such historical blunders as those above noticed, but even the most obvious typographical errors; e.g., on p. 250, under the bust of Scipio there is L., for Lucius Scipio Africanus, instead of P., for Publius Scipio Africanus; and on p. 453, footnote, we are referred to the end of chapter 37, for the bust of Ennius, when it is not there, but at the end of chapter 50, &c. Such exact faithfulness in following copy is worthy of the well-known skilfulness of the Chinese tailor, who, when about to make a new garment in European style, took home an old one for a pattern, which he succeeded in imitating with exactness, even to the patches.

Europe (for these two events are quite synchronous), I will now, as briefly as possible, give some account of the domestic life and manners of the six imperial Cæsars, who governed Rome at that period. In this account I shall enumerate their many marriages, and their numerous divorces and adoptions, and state their exact relationship to each other. By this means, I hope to be able to explain the complexity of Roman affinities, which has baffled the apprehension of so many acute and learned historians, and at the same time to exhibit the original nature and true spirit of Roman monogamy. "Ex pede Herculem;" from the Cæsars let us learn the Romans.

I should hesitate to pollute my pages with these delineations of Roman manners, if the nature of my treatise did not require it. But it is necessary to the plan and scope of this work that the analytical examination of the origin and early history of our present marriage system should be conducted with philosophical exactness, — an exactness that requires explicit facts, which I have spared no time nor labor to search out, and which I am not at liberty to withhold, however revolting they may be. In order that modern monogamists may clearly see the justice or the injustice of the boasted claims of their system to superior purity and virtue, it is very proper that they look to the rock whence they were hewn and to the hole of the pit whence they were digged.

The single family of the Cæsars is selected as an example, not because it is the worst example which those times produced, for, on the contrary, there is abundant evidence that Sylla and Catiline and Clodius and Sejanus, and the emperors Domitian and Commodus and Caracalla, and many others of their contemporaries, exceeded the Cæsars in profligacy; but the domestic history of the latter family is given, because it is the most authentic, and the most familiar to all classical and historical scholars. Caius Seutonius Tranquillus, commonly called Suetonius, is the principal authority for the facts cited; and his testimony is confirmed by all the other authorities of his own age, and fully allowed by those of every subsequent age. As he was born A.D. 70, very near the time of those whose lives he records; as he has maintained a reputation for candor and

impartiality ; as he was private secretary to the
Emperor Hadrian, and had access to the secret
archives of the Cæsars, and often alludes to their
handwriting, — no one has ever questioned either
his authenticity or his credibility.

1. JULIUS CÆSAR. — Caius Julius Cæsar, the dic-
tator, married successively four wives, whose names
were, 1. Cossutia, 2. Cornelia, 3. Pompeia, and, 4.
Calpurnia. Cossutia was a wealthy heiress, and
was married for her money ; but she was divorced
before Cæsar was eighteen years of age (which was,
according to Roman law, during the first year of
his majority), upon the occasion of the triumph of
the party of Marius, to which Cæsar had attached
himself ; when the ambitious youthful politician
and future conqueror was permitted to marry
Cornelia, the daughter of Cornelius Cinna the
consul, and the friend and colleague of Marius ;
by which alliance Cæsar brought himself at once
into public notice, and began to aspire to the
highest offices of state.   Cornelia died young,
after having given birth to Cæsar's only legitimate
child, a daughter named Julia ; who was married
to Pompey the Great, at the formation of the first

Triumvirate, but who died without issue. Pompeia, Cæsar's third wife, was divorced, in favor of Calpurnia, who survived him. He repudiated Pompeia in consequence of the affair of the infamous Clodius, who had introduced himself into Cæsar's house, disguised in female apparel, for the purpose of assailing the virtue of Pompeia, at the festival of the Bona Dea, when, by law and by custom, it was deemed the greatest sacrilege for any male to be found upon the premises. Cæsar at once divorced his wife, but brought no charge against Clodius; but he was tried for the sacrilege upon the accusation of Cicero. When Cæsar was called as a witness, and was asked why he had put away his wife, he answered with the proud remark, that his wife's chastity must not only be free from corruption, but must also be above suspicion. Yet Cæsar himself, who made this memorable remark, was excessively addicted to gross sensuality, and was the father of several illegitimate children. Suetonius says that he committed adultery with many ladies of the highest quality in Rome; among whom he specifies Posthumia the wife of Servius

Sulpitius, Lollia the wife of Aulus Gabinius, Ter-
tullia the wife of Marcus Crassus, Mutia the wife
of Pompey the Great, Eunoë the wife of Bogudes,
Cleopatra Queen of Egypt, and Servilia the
mother of Marcus Brutus, to whom he presented
a pearl costing six millions of sesterces (equal
to two hundred thirty-two thousand, one hundred
and seven dollars); at the same time seducing
her daughter Tertia. Yet in another paragraph
Suetonius says the only stain upon Cæsar's chastity
was his having committed Sodomy with Nicomedes,
King of Bithynia; which proves what has before been said, that the Romans did not consider
fornication, or even adultery, as constituting unchastity in men, but only in women; and that
they expected and permitted licentiousness in the
most respectable men, as a necessary part of their
social system of monogamy. It is evidently with
similar opinions of their social system that Dr.
Liddell thus sums up the character of Cæsar: —
" Thus died ' the foremost man in all the world,'
a man who failed in nothing that he attempted.
He might, Cicero thought, have been a great
orator: his ' Commentaries ' remain to prove that

he was a great writer. As a general, he had few
superiors ; as a statesman and politician, no equal.
His morality in domestic life was not better or
worse than commonly prevailed in those licentious
days. He indulged in profligate amours freely
and without scruple ; but public opinion reproached
him not for this. He seldom, if ever, allowed
pleasure to interfere with business, and here his
character forms a notable contrast to that of
Sylla," &c. *

2. AUGUSTUS. — He was the grand-nephew and
adopted son of Cæsar, being the grandson of his
sister Julia, wife of Marcus Atius. Their daughter,
named Atia (sometimes written Attia or Accia),
married Caius Octavius, and became the mother of
Augustus and his sister Octavia. His name, at
first, was identical with that of his father, Caius
Octavius ; but Julius Cæsar, having failed of any
direct male heir, adopted him in his last will and
testament, as his son ; and, upon the publication of the will, he assumed his adopted father's

---

* Suet. Vit. Jul. Cæsar, par. 40–50. Liddell's Hist. Rome:
London, 1857; book 7. Anthon's Class. Dict., art. "Cæsar,
Mutia," &c.

family name : twenty years afterwards the additional name or title, Augustus, was conferred upon him by vote of the Senate, and then his full name became Caius Julius Cæsar Octavianus Augustus.

Like his great-uncle, Augustus had four wives, named, 1. Servilia ; 2. Claudia ; 3. Scribonia ; and, 4. Livia Drusilla, whom he successively married and successively divorced, except the last, who survived him. And like Cæsar he had but one child — a daughter — also named Julia, who was the daughter of his third wife Scribonia. This wife he divorced soon after he obtained supreme power, and at the same time married Livia Drusilla. She was already married to Claudius Nero : she had borne her husband two sons, and was then six months advanced in pregnancy with her third child ; but Augustus demanded her on account of her beauty and accomplishments, and her husband durst not refuse the demand. She was therefore divorced from Nero, and married to Augustus. Her child was born not long afterwards, and died at birth. She was at this time twenty years of age, and highly educated. She had already travelled in foreign countries, and, to the fascinations of rare personal beauty, she added the charms of a cultivated mind.

Augustus's only child, Julia, was married three times. Her first marriage was to Marcellus, her cousin, only son of Octavia, her father's sister. Marcellus died young, much lamented, and left no issue. Augustus had, some time before, compelled Agrippa, commander-in-chief of the army, to divorce his wife Pompeia, and marry Marcella, his sister Octavia's daughter; but now, on the death of Marcellus, he commanded Agrippa to divorce his niece, Marcellus's sister, and marry his daughter, Marcellus's widow. By this second marriage, Julia had five children, three of whom were sons, the youngest of which was born after his father's death and his mother's third marriage, and was named Agrippa Posthumus: the other two sons were called Caius and Lucius. This final marriage of Julia was to Tiberius Nero, the stepson of Augustus, and was without issue: it will be alluded to again under the notice of Tiberius. Julia was one of the most dissolute women of that dissolute age. And there can be no doubt that the age and the monogamous system were even more dissolute than the women, and caused them to become so when they were not so. The chastity of the Roman matrons and virgins was prized and honored as highly by themselves, and by their husbands and fathers and brothers, as it has ever been among any people in the world ; as the legends of Lucretia and of Virginia and others can testify. The ordinances of God and of Nature in behalf of female purity were enforced among them, both by their ancient traditions and by their current laws ; and all combined to cause them to preserve their chastity to the last possible extremity. But that extremity had, with many of them, been reached. The unbounded license of the other sex, permitted by public opinion to be practised with the utmost impunity ; the scant and insufficient opportunities for lawful marriages, and the frequent, unjust, and arbitrary divorces from those marriages ; in fine, the whole theory of monogamy, — finally drove the women to desperate recklessness and ruin. It had been Julia's happy lot to be the wife of two honorable men, both eminent for their manliness, — Marcellus and Agrippa. She had also been the happy mother of five healthful children. And now, while still young, she found herself hastily and forcibly united to a man against his will; and that man a monster and a beast. It is not strange that she fell, nor that, in her fall, she dragged down many others with her. Her exalted rank easily seduced some of the noblest men of Rome to become her paramours. "And she became at length so devoid of shame and prudence as to carouse and revel openly, at night, in the Forum, and even on the Rostra. Augustus had already had a suspicion that her mode of life was not quite correct, and, when convinced of the full extent of her depravity, his anger knew no bounds. He communicated his domestic misfortune to the Senate ; he banished his dissolute daughter to the Isle of Pandateria, on the coast of Campania, whither she was accompanied by her mother Scribonia. He forbade her there the use of wine and of all delicacies in food or dress, and prohibited any person to visit her without his special permission. He caused a bill of divorce to be sent her in the name of her husband Tiberius, of whose letters of intercession for her he took no heed. He constantly rejected all the solicitations of the people for her recall ; and when, one time, they were extremely urgent, he openly prayed that they might have wives and daughters like her." Her confidential servant and freedwoman, Phœbe, having hanged herself when her mistress's profligacy was made known, Augustus declared that he would rather be the father of Phœbe than of Julia. This treatment of his daughter, and this remark concerning her, is another confirmation of the different regard had in those times to the unchaste conduct of women and of men ; for Augustus himself was a seducer and an adulterer, and was as profligate as his uncle Julius. Suetonius declares, that he constantly employed men to pimp for him, and that they took such freedom in selecting the most beautiful women for his embraces, that they compelled " both matrons and ripe virgins to strip for a complete examination of their persons." He also says, upon the authority of Marc Antony, that at an entertainment at his house, " he once took the wife of a man of consular rank from the table, in the presence of her husband, into his bedchamber, and that he brought her again to the entertainment with her ears very red and her hair in great disorder," plainly implying that every one could see that he had ravished her.

But it is the judgment of that distinguished scholar and historian, Dr. Liddell, that in these " and other less pardonable immoralities there was nothing to shock the feelings of Romans ; " and Keightley thus sums up his character. " In his public character, as sovereign of the Roman empire, few princes will be found more deserving of praise than Augustus. He cannot be justly charged with a single cruel, or even harsh action, in the course of a period of forty-four years. On the contrary, he seems in every act to have had the welfare of the people at heart. In return, never was prince more entirely beloved by all orders of his subjects ; and the title ' Father of his Country,' so spontaneously bestowed upon him, is but one among many proofs of the sincerity of their affection." " He was surrounded by no pomp ; no guards attended him ; no officers of the household were to be seen in his modest dwelling; he lived on terms of familiarity with his friends ; he appeared like any other citizen, as a witness in courts of justice, and in the senate gave his vote as an ordinary member. He was plain and simple in his mode of living, using only the most ordinary food, and wearing no clothes but what

7

were woven and made by his wife, sister, and daughter. In all his domestic relations he was kind and affectionate ; he was a mild and indulgent master, and an attached and constant friend." *

3. TIBERIUS. — Tiberius was the son of Claudius Nero and Livia Drusilla. He was not at all related by blood to the Julian family, but belonged by birth to the ancient Claudian gens ; being allied to the former family only by marriage and adoption. His mother married Augustus when he was five years of age ; he himself married Julia, Augustus's only daughter, when he was thirty ; and Augustus adopted him as his son when he was forty-five : so that he was at once the step-son, the son-in-law, and the adopted son of Augustus. His name, at first, was Tiberius Claudius Drusus Nero ; to which, after his adoption by Augustus, he added simply Cæsar. Augustus, with his characteristic prudence, as soon as he perceived that direct heirs in the male line were likely to fail him, began to make provision for the perpetuation of his name and fortune, as well as for

---

* Suet. Vit. Aug. par. 60–69 ; Liddell's Hist. of Rome, book 7 ; Keightley's Hist. Rom. Emp., chaps. 1, 2.

the preservation of the peace of the empire by making sons by adoption. He first adopted his two oldest grandsons, Caius and Lucius Agrippa, in their early childhood; but they both died during the lifetime of Augustus, and left no issue, — Lucius at the age of nineteen years; and two years afterwards, Caius, at the age of twenty-four.* Drusus Nero, the younger brother of Tiberius, and the favorite step-son of Augustus, had also died before them; but he had left two sons, Germanicus and Claudius. These with Tiberius, and his only son Drusus, by his first wife Vipsania, and Agrippa Posthumus, the only remaining son of Julia, were all the males allied to Augustus. Upon the death of Caius, therefore, A.D. 6, Augustus adopted both Agrippa Posthumus and Tiberius, and caused Tiberius at the same time to adopt Germanicus: so that all the males of the family then became Cæsars, except Claudius Nero; but he was considered foolish, and was not included. Tiberius, as has been observed,

---

* Caius married Livilla, sister to Germanicus, and grand-niece to Augustus, but had no offspring; his widow afterwards married Drusus, son of Tiberius, by whom she had two children, Tiberius and Julia.

was, at this time, forty-five years of age ; and each
of the three young men, Agrippa, Germanicus, and
Drusus, was about nineteen.

Tiberius was married twice ; first to Vipsania,
eldest daughter of Agrippa, and after divorcing her,
as usual, he married Julia, Agrippa's widow.   It
is but justice to Tiberius, to say that both the divorce and the marriage were hateful to him, and
were consummated only upon the order of Augustus.   He had lived happily with Vipsania, who was
the mother of his only son, and who was then pregnant with her second child, while Julia was also
pregnant with her fifth child by Agrippa.

Upon the death of Augustus, Tiberius commanded his step-brother Agrippa Posthumus to be put to
death, and assumed sole command of the empire.
His first order was but a sample of his government ;
for he soon became one of the most odious tyrants
that ever cursed the world.   His vices were of the
most infamous character, and comprised all that are
alluded to in the first chapter of Paul's Epistle to
the Romans, and for which the ancient city of Sodom
was destroyed by fire.   In order to give loose rein
to his worse than beastly propensities, he retired

from Rome to that lovely sequestered island in the Bay of Naples, which was then called Capreæ, and which in modern Italian is now named Capri. "But," says Keightley, "this delicious retreat was speedily converted by the aged prince into a den of infamy, such as has never, perhaps, found its equal ; and it almost chills the blood to read the details of the horrid practices in which he indulged amid the rocks of Capreæ." Like all the other Cæsars, Tiberius left no son. His son Drusus was married, and had a son and a daughter ; but he was poisoned by his own wife Livilla, and died during his father's lifetime. The grandson named Tiberius, and the grand-daughter named Julia, both survived him. His adopted son Germanicus, after achieving an excellent reputation as a man and a military commander, had also died, about five years after the accession of Tiberius, at the age of thirty-four years, attributing his death to slow poison secretly administered by the command of his adopted father. Germanicus left nine children ; but all the sons were destroyed before the death of Tiberius, except one, named Caius, but commonly called Caligula. Tiberius therefore left two male heirs only, — Caius

Caligula, his grandson by adoption, and Tiberius, his grandson by birth.*

4. Caligula. — Tiberius, by his last will, had appointed his two grandsons his joint and equal heirs; but Germanicus, the father of Caligula, had always been greatly beloved by the people, while Tiberius had been hated. The will was therefore unanimously set aside, and the sole power conferred upon Caligula. Thus was the line of the Cæsars still continued by adoption. Caligula was born A.D. 12, and became emperor at twenty-five years of age, A.D. 37. He was married four times. His wives' names were, 1. Junia Claudilla; 2. Livia Orestilla; 3. Lollia Paullina; and, 4. Milonia Cæsonia. The first died, the next two were divorced, the last survived him. Soon after the death of Junia, which was some time before he attained the supreme power, he took Ennia, the wife of Macro, as his favorite mistress, promising to procure a divorce from her husband, and to marry her himself when he should attain the empire; and Macro appears to have acquiesced in this arrangement, selling his wife's virtue and

* Suct.; Keightley; Anthon.

the honor of his house for such rewards and emoluments as Caligula was pleased to accord to him. But in the second year of his administration, instead of fulfilling his engagements to Ennia and her husband, he neglected and disgraced them; so that they both committed suicide.

Caligula then took his own sister Drusilla, and lived in incest with her, having forced her husband, Lucius Cassius, to divorce her for that purpose; but, in order to cover the affair, he caused her to be married to one of his attendants, Marcus Lepidus, his cousin, with whom he was at the same time practising the still more horrid and unnatural crime of Sodomy. Upon the death of this sister, which occurred during the same year, he mourned for her with the most extravagant grief, and caused her henceforth to be worshipped as a goddess; building a temple and consecrating priests in her honor. His own solemn oath ever after was, " By the divinity of Drusilla."

He next married Livia Orestilla; and in this strange and cruel manner. He had been invited to the wedding-feast of Caius Piso, a man belonging to one of the noblest families of Rome, whose bride was this same Livia. Caligula accepted the invitation ; the marriage ceremony took place, and the feast was at its height, when, struck with the beauty of the bride, he resolved to appropriate her to himself, and saying to Piso, " Do not touch my wife," he took her home with him. The next day he caused proclamation to be made for the information of the Roman public, that he had purveyed himself a wife after the manner of Augustus. It is not strange that under such circumstances he did not find her an agreeable consort, for her affections had been given to Piso, and with him only could she be happy. He therefore divorced her again, within three days of her marriage, but would not permit her to have her former husband.

The occasion of his marrying his next wife, Lollia Paullina, was equally strange, but quite different. He heard some one extol the beauty of her grandmother, and was inflamed with passion to enjoy hers. She was already married to Memmius Regulus, and was then away from Rome, in a foreign province, with her husband ; but Caligula sent orders to Regulus to divorce his wife, ordered her home and married her. He lived with her about a year, when he divorced her for her barrenness; and then married his last wife, Cæsonia, with whom he had already been having illicit intercourse for many months, and who was now far advanced in pregnancy. She was a woman of infamous character, and had had three illegitimate children before; but he married her, and she was very soon delivered of a daughter, which was Caligula's only child.

During most of this time, since the death of Drusilla, he was living in incest with both his other sisters, Agrippina and Livilla, while at the same time he would prostitute them to his male favorites, the ministers of his more heathenish lusts. Suetonius says, that, in addition to these incests and adulteries already specified, he debauched nearly every lady of rank in Rome; whom he was accustomed to invite, along with their husbands, to a feast: he would then examine them, as they passed his couch one after another, as one would examine female slaves when about to purchase; and after supper he would retire to his bedchamber, and then send for any lady present that he liked best.

During his administration public prostitutes paid twelve and a half per cent of their fees into the imperial treasury; and in order to increase this branch of the revenue he opened a brothel in his own palace, filled it with respectable (?) women, and sent out criers into the forum to advertise it, and invite the people to resort to it.

Caligula was slain by the officers of his own guard, in the twenty-ninth year of his age, after governing the Roman world less than four years. During the first year of his administration he had first adopted and then murdered the younger Tiberius Cæsar, then about seventeen years of age, who left no issue; and a few hours after his own death his wife Cæsonia was slain, and also their infant daughter, who had its little brains dashed out against a wall: so the last of the Cæsars seemed to have perished. But there was one old man left, who, if he was not a Cæsar, was certainly related to all the Cæsars, and it was determined to make him a Cæsar, and raise him to the supreme power. This old man was Claudius Nero.

5. CLAUDIUS. — He was the uncle of Caligula, and the nephew of Tiberius. His name at first had been Tiberius Claudius Drusus Nero, to which

he now added that of Cæsar. He was married six times. His wives' names were, 1. Æmilia Lepida; 2. Livia Medullina Camilla; 3. Plautia Urgullinilla; 4. Ælia Pætina; 5. Valeria Messalina; and, 6. Agrippina. Of these, the first, third, and fourth were divorced, the second died, the fifth was executed, and the last survived him. Ælia Pætina, the fourth, was divorced soon after Claudius obtained the empire, in order to make way for Messalina, whose principal recommendation was that she had already become pregnant by him. They were accordingly married: the child was born, and was a boy, whom they named Britannicus. She afterwards bore him a daughter called Octavia. Messalina's lust and cruelty were so unbounded, that her name has become the synonyme of every thing most vile and detestable in the female character. She has been called the Roman Jezebel; but the comparison is an injustice to the Samaritan queen. She was as much more wicked than Jezebel as Roman monogamy is more impure than Jewish polygamy. Her husband's chief officers became her adulterers, and were allied with her in all her abominations. She cast an eye of lust on the principal men in Rome, and whom she could not seduce to gratify her vile propensities she would contrive to destroy. She was so excessive in her sensuality, that she often required the services of the strongest and most vigorous men to satisfy her lusts; and often for that reason chose gladiators and slaves: but such persons would not always venture to incur the risk of discovery, and then she would make her stupid husband the unwitting broker of her adulterous pleasures. As an example of this mode of procedure, in such cases, it is recorded that " when Mnester, a celebrated dancer, refused to yield to her solicitations or her threats, she procured a written order from Claudius, commanding him to do whatever she should require. Mnester then complied. The same was the case with many others, who believed they were obeying the orders of the prince when they were yielding to the libidinous desires of his wife."

But she was not content with being infamous herself, she determined to make others so; compelling many respectable married women to prostitute themselves, even in the palace, and in the presence of their husbands, who were powerless to prevent it, for she brutally destroyed those who would not acquiesce in their wives' dishonor. Meantime her own excesses were unknown by Claudius; for she caused some one of her maids to occupy her place in his bed, and purchased by rewards, or anticipated by murder, those who could give him information. At length her enormities were discovered and brought to light in this manner, — a manner so strange and unnatural, that the grave historian Tacitus expressed his doubts whether posterity could be made to believe that any woman could be so wicked. Messalina had set her heart upon Caius Silius, the consul elect, who was esteemed the handsomest man in Rome. In order to obtain sole possession of him she drove his wife Junia out of his house; and Silius, knowing that to refuse her would be his destruction, while by compliance he might possibly escape, yielded to his fate. But the infatuated adulteress became so reckless that she disdained concealment and came openly to visit him, heaping wealth and honors upon him, and transferring the slaves and the treasures of the prince to his house. Silius then saw that he was so deep in guilt that either he or Claudius must perish, and proposed to Messalina to murder her husband and seize the supreme power. She hesitated; not from regard to her husband, but from the fear that when Silius should be invested with the empire he would cast her off. She therefore proposed, as an amendment to his plan, that they should be married first, and then murder the prince and seize the empire afterwards. This plan was agreed to; and while Claudius was absent from the city to perform a sacrifice at Ostia, when he was building the new harbor there, they were publicly married, in due form, and with much ceremony. But their own attendants were shocked. They informed the prince; and the whole plot was discovered and the guilty parties put to death.

Claudius then took for his sixth and last wife his brother's daughter Agrippina; and as such a union was regarded as incestuous by the laws and customs of the Romans, Claudius first repaired to the senate-house, and caused a new law to be passed legalizing marriages between uncles and nieces, and then formally espoused her. Agrippina, the new imperial consort, was sister to the late emperor

Caligula; and besides having lived in incest with him, she had been married twice before. By her first husband, Cneius Domitius Ahenobarbus, she had had a son, named Lucius, who was nine years of age at the time of her marriage with Claudius, and three years older than his only son Britannicus. To promote the interests of her own son Lucius, and to destroy Britannicus, was now the ruling passion of Agrippina; to gratify which she paused at nothing. Yet she was not, like Messalina, naturally inclined to licentiousness; but in order to win the influence and assistance of powerful men for promoting her ambitious designs in behalf of her son, she stooped so low as to prostitute herself to their lusts, when they could not be purchased by any other means at her command. At first she managed to have Octavia, the sister of Britannicus, divorced from Silanus, to whom she had been betrothed, and married to her son Lucius, and, in a year or two afterwards, to have Lucius adopted by Claudius as his son. Three years afterwards she procured poison from the notorious Locusta, and put her husband, the Emperor Claudius, to death, in the sixty-fourth year of his age, after he had governed Rome a little less than fourteen years.*

6. NERO. — Agrippina carefully concealed the death of Claudius until secure measures had been taken for setting aside Britannicus, and for the succession of her son; when the death was announced and the new emperor proclaimed. Nero was successively the grand-nephew, the step-son, the son in-law, and the adopted son of Claudius; and, by adoption, the great-grandson of Tiberius; being son of Agrippina, daughter of Germanicus, adopted son of Tiberius. He was also, by birth, the grand-nephew of Augustus, by the collateral female line; his father, Domitius Ahenobarbus, being son of Antonia Major, eldest daughter of Octavia, sister of Augustus. His name, at first, was Lucius Domitius Ahenobarbus; but upon his adoption by Claudius, into the Julian family, he took the name of Nero Claudius Cæsar.

He was married seven times. The names of his consorts were, 1. Octavia; 2. Poppæa Sabina; 3. Octavia again; 4. Poppæa again; 5. Statilia Mes-

---

* Suet. Vit. Claud.; Tacitus Ann.; Keight.; Anthon.

salina; 6. Sporus; and, 7. Doryphorus. It will readily be seen, from this list, that his marriages and divorces were more numerous than his brides, and that the last two names are those of males.

Nero had no affection for his first wife, the chaste and modest Octavia, whom he had married from policy, and not for love: and his mother, the ambitious Agrippina, who loved power so much, was pleased with this indifference; for she hoped to maintain an undivided influence over him, and through him to rule the world. But in the second year of his administration he conceived a violent passion for an Asiatic freedwoman named Acte; a passion which his preceptor, the celebrated philosopher Seneca, and his other councillors of state, encouraged; permitting him to take her as his acknowledged mistress, without rebuke, hoping that this attachment would keep him from a life of promiscuous licentiousness and from debauching women of rank. But Agrippina was furious; not because Acte was a low-bred woman (though this was the excuse for her opposition), but she felt that her own power would be diminished by her: and she threatened that if he did not give her up, she

8

would herself abandon him, and would set up Britannicus; and, as the daughter of the beloved Germanicus, would appeal to the army against her son, in Britannicus' behalf. This was a powerful argument, and Nero knew that his mother was capable of any thing to maintain her power; but he resolved, that, instead of giving up his mistress, he would murder his innocent brother. He procured poison from Locusta and gave it him, but it proved too weak; he then sent for Locusta again, and reproached her and beat her, and bade her prepare a stronger dose. She obeyed him; and, having proved the potency of the venom upon a kid and a pig, he had it given to Britannicus, in some cold water, at dinner. Its effect was instantaneous, and the poor boy dropped down dead. Nero carelessly remarked to the company that he had been subject to fits from infancy, and would soon recover. Agrippina and Octavia were struck with terror, and said nothing; the latter, young as she was, having learned to suppress her feelings, and the former perceiving that her son was fast becoming her superior both in cruelty and in craft.

Nero next became enamored of Poppæa Sabina,

a lady of great beauty and of noble birth, who had been divorced from her first husband, Crispinus, and was then married to her second, Marcus Otho; but Otho was sent out as governor of the distant province of Portugal, and Nero gave himself up to the enjoyment of his adulterous passion. Then Agrippina became more furious than ever, for she saw, that if he should divorce Octavia, and marry Poppæa, her own influence would be gone forever. But she set at work in a different manner than before; for such was her insane love of power, that, in order to retain her influence over her son, she began herself to pander to his vices, diverting and distracting his mind with a succession of beautiful ladies, offering her purse, and the use of her own apartments for his private assignations, and even attempting to seduce him to unnatural incest with herself; and nothing but the fear of the army and of the people prevented them from the consummation of that abominable crime. Still the influence of Poppæa increased; and so did Agrippina's hatred and jealousy of her, until at length Nero resolved upon the crime of matricide, which he effected in

the most barbarous manner. He first attempted
to drown her, in a manner that might appear
accidental, by sending her to sea in an unsea-
worthy vessel laden with lead; the deck of which
was to give way at the proper time, and the
vessel itself to fall in pieces. She went on board,
and the deck fell, with its freight of lead, as was
expected; but she was saved by the devotion of
her attendants. He then sent assassins to shed
her blood. When they entered her apartment,
and one of them drew his sword, she exposed her
womb, and cried out, " Strike here : " he obeyed,
and thus she perished. But it was only after the
lapse of three years more, that he divorced the
virtuous Octavia, by whose alliance he had obtained the empire, and who was greatly beloved
by the people. He effected her divorce, however,
and married Poppæa; but the murmurs of the
people were so alarming, that, in a short time, he
divorced Poppæa, and married Octavia the second
time. But his affections were still unchanged,
and he at length induced Anicetus, the assassin
that had slain his mother, to make oath that
Octavia had committed adultery with him; and,

although nobody believed the wretch, this served as a pretext for divorcing her again. She was then banished to the usual place, the Island of Pandataria, where she was soon afterwards put to death, at twenty-one years of age, and her head sent as a present to Poppæa; to whom Nero was then married the second time. Soon after this marriage, to his great joy, she bore him a daughter, his first and only child, which lived, however, but a few months.

It was the next year after the birth of this infant, that Rome was burnt [A.D. 65]. The loss of lives, as well as of property, was very great. The streets of the city were narrow and crooked, and the flames spread so rapidly, that escape was difficult. The fire raged six days. Five-sevenths of the city was laid waste. Nero has often been charged with having caused the fires himself; but the charge has never been proved. He was strongly suspected at the time, and, in order to divert suspicion from himself, he laid the blame upon the innocent Christians. They had become already numerous in the city, and were generally hated and despised. They were put to death, upon this suspicion, with torture and insult; some torn to pieces by dogs, after being sewed up in the skins of wild animals, some crucified, and some wrapped in pitch and set on fire, to serve for lamps in the night. Two years after the great fire, Poppæa came to her death in as brutal a manner as mother, sister, and brother had done before. She was killed by Nero, in a fit of anger, by a violent kick when in an advanced state of pregnacy.

He then celebrated his fifth marriage, with a lady named Messalina; with whom it happened to be her fifth marriage also. Her last husband was Atticus Vestinus, whom Nero put to death in order to obtain possession of his wife. But he soon divorced her, yet that did not break her heart, for she outlived him, and preserved her beauty to captivate the fancy of another emperor, in future years.

Nero was married the sixth time to a boy. His name was Sporus. Nero fancied that his beauty resembled that of his slain Poppæa, whose death he repented and bewailed. He caused Sporus to be made a eunuch, and exhausted the powers of art in trying to make him a woman. He then espoused him, with the most solemn forms of marriage; and it was cleverly remarked by the people, that it was a great pity that his father Domitius had not had such a wife.

His seventh and last marriage was to Doryphorus, his own freedman; but in this case Nero himself was the bride, and his manumitted slave the groom. Nero was a musician and a comedian, and was accustomed to spend a great part of his time in rehearsal and in public performance, as an actor. He chose the crowded theatre as the place in which to celebrate this marriage. He first covered himself with the skin of a wild beast, and in that dress, before thousands of assembled men and women, committed rapes upon persons of both sexes, who were tied to stakes for that purpose. Having thus demonstrated his manhood, he appeared as the bride in his marriage to Doryphorus, to whom he was married in the same solemn form that Sporus had been married to him: finishing the representation by consummating the marriage in the embraces of Doryphorus, himself imitating the cries and shrieks of young virgins when they are ravished.

Nero died by his own hand, A.D. 68, in the thirty-first year of his age, and the fourteenth of his imperial power. He left no child, either by birth or by adoption. He was the last of the Cæsars. That name was henceforth only an honorary title. Can any one regret the extinction of the dissolute and degenerate race? Is it not a happy provision in the laws of God, that " monsters cannot propagate "? *

Such was monogamy at the commencement of the Christian era ; for it was during the reign of Augustus that Christ was born, and during that of Nero that Paul was beheaded. Such was the social system imposed by Rome upon the nations of Europe. This is no fancy sketch, nor have the facts here cited been herein exaggerated. My authorities are accessible to every scholar, and I invite criticism and investigation. The question now arises, How was Roman monogamy affected by its contact with Christianity? And this question I shall proceed to discuss in another chapter.

---

* Sueton. Vit. Neronis, par. 20–29. ; Tac. Ann.; Keight. Hist. Rom. Emp.

CHAPTER VI.

HOW WAS ROMAN MONOGAMY AFFECTED BY THE INTRODUCTION OF CHRISTIANITY?

THE introduction of Christianity effected no violent revolutions of any kind in the social relations of men and women, except by purifying these relations, and enforcing the duties dependent upon them. Christianity did not dictate any particular form of government, or any code of laws, but enjoined obedience to the existing laws, when they were not inconsistent with the laws of the gospel. The first Christians, while they were themselves scarcely tolerated, were not inclined to attempt a social revolution by opposing the established system of monogamy; but they attempted to oppose only its vices, and to remove them. They insisted, from the first, upon purity and chastity in men and women equally. They denounced prostitution, adultery, and frequent and

capricious divorces, and did what they could to
eradicate their practice.   But before they attained
any degree of civil or religious freedom, or were
in any situation to introduce the purer system of
polygamy, they had themselves become thoroughly
Romanized ; and the errors of Gnosticism, Platonism, and Montanism had then prevailed so extensively as to impel them, at last, to attempt a social
reformation in a direction quite contrary to polygamy, by discouraging marriage, and by introdu-
cing asceticism, monasticism, and celibacy.

GNOSTICISM IN THE FIRST CENTURY.

Christianity was not fully tolerated in Europe
till the time of the Emperor Constantine the
Great, in the former part of the fourth century ;
and was not established by law as the religion of
Rome, till the reign of Theodosius, in the very
last part of that century ; while Gnosticism and its
cognate errors began to be disseminated even in the
first century, in apostolic times : they prevailed
extensively in the second century, and had permanently corrupted the church in the third and
fourth.   While the different Gnostic writers and

teachers differed greatly from one another on many points of belief, they were generally agreed in their fundamental doctrines, which sprung from the ancient Persian or Magian system of religion, and which taught the existence of two eternal beings, — Ormuzd, or God, the author of good, and the creator of light, which is his emblem; and Ahriman, or the Devil, the author of evil, and the creator of darkness, his emblem. They believed that the world consisted of spirit and of matter, both being eternal; the latter, essentially evil, formed or moulded by the Devil from the eternal substance of chaos, and the former, essentially good, proceeding out of God, and still forming a part of God: hence, that the body is vile, wicked, and dark; while the soul is pure, holy, and light. The body, therefore, with its appetites and passions, should be despised and subdued; while the soul, with its superior attributes, should be cherished and obeyed. The principal Gnostic teachers of the first century were Simon Magus, Menander, and Cerinthus. They all studied at Alexandria, and all became Christians. Cerinthus taught that the man Jesus

was born of Joseph and Mary in the natural way;
that the εἰῶν, Christ, descended on him at his baptism, in the form of a dove ; and, previous to the
crucifixion, that the εἰῶν returned to God, leaving
the man to suffer on the cross.

GNOSTICISM AND PLATONISM OF THE SECOND CENTURY.

In the second century, the Gnostic Christians
became much more numerous and influential.
Among the writers and teachers whom historians
particularly mention were Saturninus, Basilides,
Carpocrates, Valentine, Bardesanes, Tatian, Mar-
cion, Montanus, Tertullian, and Origen. Saturninus
(A.D. 115) taught that Satan, the ruler of matter, was coeval with the Deity ; that the world was
created by seven angels, without the knowledge
of the Deity, who, however, was not displeased
when he saw it, and breathed into man a rational
soul. Satan, enraged at the creation of the world
and the virtue of its inhabitants, formed another
race of men out of matter, with malignant souls
like his own ; and hence arose the great moral
difference to be observed among men. The moral

discipline of Saturninus was ascetic and severe:
he discouraged marriage, declaring it to be the doctrine of the Devil; * he enjoined abstinence from
wine and flesh, and taught to keep under the body,
as being formed from matter, which is in its
essence evil and corrupt. Bardesanes wrote about
A.D. 170, in the time of the Emperor Marcus
Aurelius. " His moral system was ascetic in the
extreme; he enjoined his disciples to renounce
wedlock, abstain from animal food, and live in
solitude on the slightest and most meagre diet, and
even to use water instead of wine in the Lord's
Supper." † Montanus (A.D. 175) insisted upon
more frequent and more rigorous fasts than had
yet prevailed in the church, for they had hitherto
fasted only during the passion-week; he forbade
second marriages; taught the absolute and irrevo-
cable excommunication of adulterers, murderers,
and idolaters; required all chaste women to wear
veils; and forbade all kinds of costly attire and
ornaments of the person. His most distinguished
disciple was Tertullian, bishop of Carthage, a

---

* Mosheim, Ecc. Hist., vol. 1, p. 246.

† Keightley's Hist. Rom. Emp., part 2, chap. 7.

very learned and voluminous writer, whose works
have been held in the greatest estimation in every
age. Origen, a still more learned and more voluminous writer, and a very eloquent preacher,
embraced the Gnostic errors when a young man,
and carried his principles of subduing the passions
of the body to such an extent, that he made a
eunuch of himself: but in after-life, when he had
spent many years in studying, translating, and ex-
pounding the Holy Scriptures, and understood
them better, he regretted the rash act of his youth,
and greatly modified his Gnostic sentiments; so
much so, that many have accused him of teaching
different views of the same subject, and of con-
tradicting himself.

The first Platonic philosopher who joined the
Christians was Justin Martyr, who was beheaded
at Rome A.D. 155; followed by Clement of Alexandria, A.D. 192, who had a school in that city
called the Catechetic School, which attempted to
harmonize the philosophy of Plato with the mate-
rialism of the Gnostics by means of the common
medium of Christianity. This scheme was called
the New Platonism; and a long contest prevailed

between the followers of this system and the advocates for gospel simplicity. But the victory appeared to be on the side of the Platonists, which assured the lasting corruption of Christianity ; for learned Christians now began to maintain that the Scriptures have a double meaning ; one literal and plain, and the other latent and symbolic : the literal or exoteric sense to be taught to the people, and the latent or esoteric sense to be communicated only to the initiated and the faithful. A similar distinction in morals followed. There was one rule for the multitude, and another for the aspirants to higher sanctity. These were to seek retirement and to mortify the flesh, avoiding marriage and all indulgence of the senses. Hence originated the austerities of religious hermits ; hence the celibacy of priests, monks, and nuns.

RELATION OF MONOGAMY TO CHRISTIANITY IN THE THIRD AND FOURTH CENTURIES.

At the council of Cæsarea, A.D. 314, it was decided and decreed, in the first canon, that, if a priest should marry after his ordination, he must be deposed from office. The seventh canon forbids a priest to be present at the marriage of a bigamist.

At the council of Ancyra, in the same year, it was ordered, in the tenth canon, that those deacons who expressed their intention to marry at the time of their ordination might innocently do so ; but, if they should marry without having expressed such intention, they must be deposed from office.

At the first council of Carthage, A.D. 348, by the second canon, it was ordered that all Christians who had violated their vows of virginity by subsequent marriage should be excommunicated ; and, if they were priests, they should be deposed from office.

Siricius, Bishop of Rome, in 385 ordered that every priest and every deacon within his diocese who should marry a second wife, or a widow, should be deposed from office.

While these Gnostic and Platonic sentiments were at work corrupting the church within, the state of social life without the pale of Christianity was much the same as it has been described under the first six Cæsars ; or, if the testimony of all the contemporary writers can be believed, it was becoming more and more corrupt. The Christians formed but a small minority of the whole population, and they were generally hated, and often persecuted. It is scarcely possible for us to conceive of any greater depravity than that of the age of Caligula and Nero ; and we do not wonder to learn that in the succeeding century the once mighty Roman empire was beginning to totter to its fall. But before it fell it was destined to be upheld a while by the fortitude of Christian patriots ; and, in turn, the purity of Christianity was to become more and more sullied by its long contact with Roman depravity, and its intimate complicity with Roman monogamy.

CONSTANTINE AND THEODOSIUS.

In the former part of the fourth century, the two joint emperors were Constantine and Licinius. They agreed, at first, to tolerate Christianity ; but Licinius violated his agreement, and commenced a persecution. Then Constantine, who had himself been a pagan hitherto, resolved to favor the Christians more than he had done already, and thus attach to himself the most industrious and peaceable citizens, and the most brave and loyal soldiers

9

of the empire. In the year A.D. 324 the cross appeared for the first time upon his banners; his rival was defeated, and he became sole emperor. Then Constantine issued circular letters, announcing his conversion to Christianity, and inviting the people to follow his example. This call of the powerful monarch was not unheeded. The Christian faith spread rapidly : ministers of religion thronged the royal court, and offices of honor and profit were conferred upon Christians. Yet Constantine himself, through all his subsequent life, was only a catechumen or inquirer, and was not baptized, and received into full membership in the church, until he was near his end. And, in the mean time, he left the ancient system of the Roman state undisturbed ; and paganism, with its corrupt monogamy, was still the law of the land. At length Theodosius, his grandson, required the Senate, a majority of whom had hitherto remained pagans, to choose between the two religions ; and they were finally induced to vote in accordance with his wishes, in favor of Christianity. He soon (A.D. 392) published a severe edict against paganism ; and " then pretended conversions became numerous, the temples were deserted, and the churches filled with worshippers, and the religion under which Rome flourished for twelve centuries ceased forever." *

ASCETICISM AND MONASTICISM.

And then at length, when Christianity became paramount in the State, a permanent and decided social reform might have been possible, had they tolerated polygamy, as the first Christians had done in Judæa and other Asiatic countries; for they would thus have made it possible for all to be married that wished to marry, and thus have guarded themselves from the terrible licentiousness of the pagans, by the influences of which they were surrounded on every hand. But, on the contrary, impelled by the prevailing influences of Gnosticism, they not only retained their former monogamy, but they made it more strict and ascetic than before, and attempted an impossible reform by suppressing the amorous propensities, and vainly endeavoring to eradicate them. The bishops and doctors of the church had already done what they could to discourage marriage, and bring it into disrepute, es-

---

* Keightley, Rom. Emp., part 3, chap. 6.

pecially with the ministers of religion ; but now they forbade it to them altogether.

At the council of Toledo, in A.D. 400, it was ordered, by canon seventeenth, that every Christian that had both a wife and a concubine should be excommunicated ; but he should not be excommunicated who had only a concubine without a wife.

At the fourth council of Carthage, A.D. 401, it was ordered, by canon seventieth, that all bishops, priests, and deacons, who had wives, must repudiate them, and live in celibacy, under penalty of deposition from office.

Pope Innocent I., about A.D. 412, in his official letter to the two bishops of Abruzzo, orders them to depose those priests who had been guilty of the crime of having children since their ordination.

Thus the seeds of Gnostic error, that had been sown in the church during the former periods of its history, now sprang up anew, and bore a plentiful harvest.   " Nothing," says Keightley, " is more characteristic of the corruption which Christianity had undergone than the high honor in which the various classes of ascetics were held.   These useless or pernicious beings now actually swarmed

throughout the Eastern empire, and were gradually spreading themselves into the West. We
have shown how asceticism has been derived from
the sultry regions of Asia, and how it originates
in the Gnostic principles. It had long been insinu-
ating itself into the church ; but, after the establishment of Christianity, it burst forth like a torrent."
" The hope of acquiring heaven by virginity and
mortification was not confined to the male sex :
woman, with the enthusiasm and the devotional
tendency peculiar to her, rushed eagerly towards
the crown of glory. Nunneries became numerous,
and were thronged with inmates. Nature, however, not unfrequently asserted her rights ; and the
complaints and admonitions of the most celebrated
fathers assure us that the unnatural state of vowed
celibacy was productive of the same evils and scandals in ancient as in modern times." *

MEDIÆVAL SUPERSTITION AND IMMORALITY.

" And then," says the learned ecclesiastical historian, Mosheim, " the number of immoral and un-

---

* Hist. Rom. Emp., chap. 6.

worthy Christians began so to increase, that the
examples of real piety and virtue became extremely rare.   When the terrors of persecution
were totally dispelled; when the church, secured
from the efforts of its enemies, enjoyed the sweets
of prosperity and peace; when the major part of
its bishops exhibited to their flocks the contagious
examples of arrogance, luxury, effeminacy, ani-
mosity, and strife, with other vices too numerous to
mention; when multitudes were drawn into the
profession of Christianity, not by the power of conviction and argument, but by the prospect of gain
or by the fear of punishment, — then it was indeed
no wonder that the church was contaminated with
shoals of profligate Christians, and that the virtuous few were, in a manner, oppressed and over-
whelmed by the superior numbers of the wicked
and licentious."   " Nor did the evil end here; for
those vain fictions, which an attachment to the
Platonic philosophy and to popular opinions had
engaged the greatest part of the Christian doctors
to adopt before the time of Constantine, were now
confirmed, enlarged, and embellished in various
ways.   Hence arose the extravagant veneration

for departed saints, the celibacy of priests, the worship of images and relics, which, in process of time, almost totally destroyed the Christian religion, or at least eclipsed its lustre, and corrupted its essence." " A preposterous desire of imitating the pagan rites, and of blending them with the Christian worship, and that idle propensity which the generality of mankind have towards a gaudy and ostentatious religion, all combined to establish the reign of superstition on the ruins of Christianity. Accordingly, frequent pilgrimages were undertaken to Palestine and to the tombs of the martyrs, as if there alone the sacred principles of virtue and the certain hope of salvation were to be acquired. The public processions and supplications, by which the pagans endeavored to appease their gods, were now adopted into the Christian worship, and celebrated with great pomp and magnificence. The virtues that had formerly been ascribed to the heathen temples, to their lustrations, to the statues of their gods and heroes, were now attributed to the Christian churches, to water consecrated by certain forms of prayer, to the images of holy men; and the worship of the martyrs was modelled according to the religious services that were paid to the gods before the coming of Christ." *

Similar testimonies could easily be cited from Gibbon's " Decline and Fall of the Roman Empire," from D'Aubigne's " History of the Reformation," from the ancient works of Eusebius, and the modern ones of Neander, and from hundreds of others ; but I will not weary my readers with them. Thus it appears from the testimonies of all the historians, ecclesiastical and civil, sacred and profane, that the doctrines and practices which distinguish the Roman-Catholic Church to-day were most of them derived from a very early age, anterior to the civil acknowledgment and legal establishment of Christianity. Keightley says, " The Church of Rome is, in fact, very unjustly treated when she is charged with being the author of the tenets and practices which were transmitted to her from the fourth century. Her guilt or error was not that of invention, but of retention."

IMMUTABILITY OF THE ROMAN CHURCH.

Her boasted claim of immutability is well sustained, as far back, certainly, as the commence-

---

* Mosheim, Ecc. Hist. Cent. 4, part 2, chap. 3.

ment of the fifth century. The Western empire
survived till the close of that century; and as the
power of the emperors continued to decline, that of
the bishops of Rome, who were afterwards called
popes, continued to increase, till at length they attained monarchical as well as hierarchical power,
and governed the religious and the social affairs of
the European world. And as the dogmas of the
Roman Church are now maintaining monogamy
with many of its attendant vices, and are now pro-
hibiting marriage to its clergy, and discouraging it
in all its more earnest religious devotees, of both
sexes, so they always have done. And we have the
testimonies of all modern historians, all modern
travellers, and of modern statistics, that the vices
of old Rome that then attended its social system of
monogamy are still the vices of modern Rome, and
of all the countries under the sway of the Roman
Church; the most recent statistics of the Catholic
countries of Europe giving the number of illegitimate children born there each year, as greater
than the number of those of legitimate birth. And
it is not only on the corrupt soil of old Europe that
the licentiousness of ancient Roman monogamy

still prevails, but also in the Catholic countries of new America. In proof of this I will cite only one testimony, where thousands might be cited, from a recent work entitled " What I saw in South and North America." By H. W. Baxley, M.D., Special Commissioner of the United-States Government. D. Appleton & Co., New York, 1865. This is his description of " what he saw " in Lima, the capital of Peru : —

" It is rarely the case that one walks in any part of the city, during the day or night, without being shocked by sights of indecency, immodesty, and immorality, too gross even to be hinted at, and disgraceful to the arrogant civilization of the nation. If one thousand seven hundred and ninety-three priests, exercising ecclesiastical authority and performing religious functions in this city, as published in its statistics, with seventy churches, forty-two chapels, six hundred and twenty-eight altars, and vast power of influence and enforcement, cannot produce a better state of morals and manners, it shows either a defective system of religion, or incapacity and faithlessness on the part of the executors of the holy trust. The statements of candid citizens and of foreign residents of many years compel the belief, that the general demoralization is mainly due to a depraved clergy. If priests taking vows of chastity and devotion alone to God, perjure themselves, obey the lusts of the flesh, and scatter their illegitimate offspring abroad, it is to be expected that they will find imitators among those whose temporal purity they should guard, and whose eternal welfare they should promote. The unblushing boldness with which clerical debauchery stalks abroad in Lima renders it needless to put in any saving clause of declaration. The priest may be seen on the sabbath day, as on others, in bull-ring and cock-pit, restaurant and tavern, with commoner and concubine, joining in noisy revel, or looking on with complacent sanction. Nor does the going-down of the sun arrest his wayward peregrinations; for he may be seen at that hour, at corners, with *tapadas*, in gay and lascivious conversation, or threading by-ways in fulfilment of a lustful assignation. If the bishop of Arequipas will turn to the ' weak and beggarly elements of the world,' if he cannot, like his great predecessor St. Paul, ' contain,' but must obey the carnal desires, ' let him marry,' as he is commanded by the apostle, like an honorable man and a consistent Christian; and let him not encourage the frailty of depraved disciples by a shameless example of licentiousness made public by his procurement of separate apartments in Lima for his seven concubines and his thirty-five illegitimate children.

" The streets of this capital were yesterday the scene of a procession which was a disgrace to its professed enlightenment, and an idolatrous violation of its boasted Christianity. A gorgeously-gilded throne, borne on the shoulders of negroes, who were partially concealed by a deep valance, supported the pontifically-attired effigy of St. Peter ; its right arm, moved by secret machinery, being occasionally raised in attitude of blessing the throngs of deluded worshippers who bowed their heads for its benediction. Another similarly decorated dais bore a life-size graven image of La Merced, the patron saint of Peru ; elegantly arrayed in curls, coronet, richly-embroidered crinoline and robe, pearl necklace and ear-rings, brooch and bodice ; and holding in its uplifted jewelled fingers a silver *yoke*. These effigies were escorted by prelates and other ecclesiastics ; and that of La Merced was preceded by six pert-looking mulatto girls, — designed to represent virgins, — carrying incense upon silver salvers, from which numerous censers, swung by priestly hands, were kept supplied, and rolled upward their clouds of perfume, to tell of the adoration of her votaries. The whole procession moved to the sound of measured chants sung by hundreds of the clergy, who often bowed ; behind whom followed the civic dignitaries of the nation and city, bareheaded and reverential; and after these came the plumed warriors, on horse and foot, with breastplate and helmet, lance, sabre, musket, and cannon, flaunting banners, and martial music, guarding the saints through the city, and back to the altars of the Church of La Merced, whence they came, and where they will receive hereafter, as heretofore, the petitions and vows of thousands of misguided religionists. Can popular regeneration be rationally looked for when examples of ecclesiastical profligacy are patent to the public eye, and when such violations of divine precepts are practised, and such delusions devised to mislead the ignorant?

"No one can scrutinize the social habits in Lima, without becoming sensible of the fact that women are probably 'more sinned against than sinning.' For they not only have provocations to faithlessness, and opportunity afforded for its indulgence by sanctioned customs, but they are taught by the universally-recognized dissoluteness of the men not to place any confidence in them, and not to contemplate marriage as a means of happiness beyond its power to furnish an establishment, and make a woman mistress of her own actions.

"In the street called San Francisco, opposite the monastery of that name, a kind of barracks is found, containing quite a population apart from the rest. There lives a class of women and children whom one would think came in a direct line from the gypsies, if their complexion did not show a variety of a thousand shades, from white to black. These women are the acknowledged mistresses, and the children the progeny, of the monks, who visit them at all times, and pay them a regular stipend. 'La casa de la monjas,' — the house of the nuns, — as the people ironically call it, is a real Gomorrah. The clerical protectors of the tenants that inhabit it willingly mistake the chambers, not having the weakness of the laity of being jealous of each other. Do not suppose that we are amusing ourselves in speaking ill of the monks of Lima. These abominations among themselves they are the first to expose; for in their stated elections for superiors, such is the bitterness of rival aspirants, that they publicly charge against each other these infamous transactions, making known the number of their concubines and illegitimate children."

Thus have Dr. Baxley and others cast the principal reproach of this frightful immorality upon the poor priests; but does it not belong rather to their entire social system? The priests in assuming the vows of perpetual celibacy, and the people in supporting the old Roman monogamy, which their Gnostic views of Christianity require, have assumed more than human nature is able to bear, and more than it ought to bear; and there must be constant transgression and immorality as long as their present system prevails.

And now I think I have fairly demonstrated that the European social system of monogamy had its origin in Roman paganism, and has been perpetuated by Roman Catholicism.

CHAPTER VII.

MONOGAMY AS IT IS AMONG PROTESTANTS.

MONOGAMY IS ROMANISM STILL.

TAKE monogamy as it is to-day, in Protestant countries, and we see that the old Roman leaven is still in it. Christianity has not reformed and purified that system so much as that has corrupted Christianity. Most of us in these countries are accustomed to congratulate ourselves upon our happy escape from the bondage and the bigotry of the Papal Church. But we are mistaken. We have not escaped. Rome binds us in stronger shackles than the iron chains of the holy Inquisition. Her shackles are upon our consciences : they are intertwined with every fibre of our social life. Much of her intolerant spirit, many of her questionable doctrines and practices, and her traditional forms and ceremonies, are still common to the nominally Christian world. In respect to a few of them, we have discovered that they are unscriptural, and unsupported by divine authority, and are therefore of no binding obligation ; but, by many other traditional doctrines and practices of that hierarchy, we are unconsciously, and therefore so much the more securely fettered. We boast of our Christian freedom, while we are, in fact, but little better than slaves ; for if we are nomially free, yet we are bound by an apprenticeship to Rome more degrading than our former slavery itself : and our boasted emancipation is but a miserable farce. We are too servile and timid in our interpretation of the Bible, and in our examination of the divine and natural laws. We hesitate to follow the simple truth to its legitimate and logical conclusions. We stand aghast at the radical changes which severe truth requires in our religious and social systems. We shrink from exploring the profound labyrinths to which truth attempts in vain to lead us ; while we look anxiously around for clews and leading-strings by which to trace our way. We dare not go forward without example and authority ; and authority and example are reconducting us to Rome.

Our great champion, Dr. Martin Luther, made a few bold steps in the right direction, but stopped far short of the ultimate results to which his own principles were leading. A Protestant in theory, he was, in practice, essentially a Romanist. He insisted much upon justification by faith alone, and declared personal piety to be necessary to true Christianity; and yet he admitted all citizens, irrespective of their faith or their want of it, to the most solemn and most esoteric ordinances of the Christian Church. He repudiated the authority of earthly potentates to compel men's Christian belief, but retained the union of Church and State in order to compel their Christian obedience. He denied the infallibility of the pope, and the miraculous power of the priesthood, and yet believed in the Real Presence, if not the adoration of the host. His disciples are to-day imitating his example rather than promoting his principles, and possess little more evangelical faith than the Romanists themselves.

Henry the Eighth, the founder of the Church of England, was even less a Protestant than Luther; and the present tendency of many of the most influential doctors and dignitaries of this Church is in the same retrograde direction as that of the Lutherans. Yet these two churches, the Anglican and the Lutheran, are the main pillars of Protestantism, — the Boaz and Jachin of the porch of the new temple. I have not lost my hope that the truth of gospel simplicity will ultimately prevail over ecclesiastical bigotry; but it may require as many centuries for the Christian world to unlock the trammels of the Roman hierarchy, and to escape from its thraldom, as it originally required to fix those trammels upon the consciences of Christian freemen.

But the Romans are more consistent in their system of monogamy than we are; for while the dogmas of the Church forbid polygamy, and even single marriages to the ministry, they provide for the surplus women, by having numerous societies of nuns and sisters of charity, who make a merit of necessity, by assuming the vows of perpetual celibacy, to serve the Church, and acquire religious merit. As Protestants, we have been taught to believe that these monastic institutions have proved to be schools of vice, and that the vows of perpetual chastity assumed in them are unnatural and wicked, and that they are often violated under the detestable hypocrisy of sacerdotal sanctity.*   For

---

* The following citations are from Froude's Hist. of Eng., vol. ii., chap. 10.

"Only light reference will be made in this place to the darker scandals by which the abbeys were dishonored. Such things there really were, to an extent which it may be painful to believe, but which evidence too abundantly proves:"

Among other specifications, Mr. Froude cites the letter of the Archbishop of Canterbury (written A.D. 1489) to the Abbot of St. Albans, wherein he accuses him thus: "'Not a few of your fellow monks and brethren, as we most deeply grieve to learn, giving themselves over to a reprobate mind, laying aside the fear of God, do lead only a life of lasciviousness, — nay, as is horrible to relate, be not afraid to defile the holy places, even the very churches of God, by infamous intercourse with nuns. You yourself, moreover, among other grave enormities and abominable crimes whereof you are guilty, and for which you are noted and diffamed, have, in the first place, admitted a certain married woman named Elena Germyn, who has separated herself, without just cause, from her husband, and for some time past has lived in adultery with another man, to be a nun, or sister in the Priory of Bray; and . . . Father Thomas Sudbury, one of your brother monks, publicly, notoriously, and without interference or punishment from you, has associated and still associates with this woman, as an adulterer with his harlot. Moreover, divers other of your brethren and fellow-

these reasons, we have suppressed the nunneries; but we have made no provision for the nuns, and those who would have become nuns. In those institutions they were, at least, assured of a home and a support, even if they did learn vice; but now, when thrown upon the world, they are still more exposed to vice, and are without a home and without support. Under Catholic monogamy, if a young woman made a false step, she could hide

---

monks have resorted and do resort continually to her and other women at the same place, as to a public brothel or receiving house. Nor is Bray the only house into which you have introduced disorder. At the Nunnery of Sapwell, you depose those who are good and religious, you promote to the highest dignities the worthless and the vicious.' "

In the year 1536, the Report of Special Commissioners appointed to inspect the Monasteries of England was laid before parliament, by which it appeared, says Mr. Froude, that "two-thirds of the monks in England were living in habits which may not be described. . . . The case against the monasteries was complete; and there is no occasion either to be surprised or peculiarly horrified at the discovery. The demoralization which was exposed was nothing less and nothing more than the condition into which men of average nature compelled to celibacy, and living as the exponents of a system which they disbelieved, were certain to fall."

her shame in a convent, and devote her future life to penitence and prayer; but, under Protestant monogamy, the frail fair sinner has no such refuge. Her first lapse from virtue shuts her out forever from the respect and sympathy of the world, and from the hope of future reformation; and her downward career to the gates of hell is so generally taken for granted, that it becomes almost a certainty. The only safe and proper provision for homeless women is marriage. An early marriage will usually save them from the dangers to which they are exposed. Monogamy cannot secure their marriage; but polygamy can: yet we are taught to look with horror upon polygamy as one of the " relics of barbarism," although it is plainly taught in the Bible, and is the only social system which provides marriage for all, and which secures the honest and lawful gratification of those impetuous passions which must be and which will be indulged in some manner, if not by marriage, then without it; while we wink at all the disgusting abominations of prostitution, divorce, adultery, and other vices, which are the well-known and the inevitable results of restricted marriage. Monogamy, in "forbidding to marry," assumes all the curses which this prohibition entails. We must choose between the system which provides marriage for all, with comparative purity, or the system of restricted marriage with inevitable impurity.

IMPURITY OF MODERN MONOGAMY.

The Bible forbids prostitution, but permits polygamy. The ancient Greeks and Romans forbade polygamy, but permitted prostitution. Modern monogamy pretends to forbid both, but really permits prostitution also. Our monogamous morality is, therefore, that of ancient paganism, and not that of the Bible; and prostitution is as much a necessary part of our social system as it was of that at Athens, at Corinth, or at Rome. Our magistrates are not ignorant of the extent of public licentiousness; but they do not attempt to suppress it. They only seek to conceal it, and confine it, if possible, within its present limits, requiring its votaries to keep it in the dark. Our police-officers know almost every prostitute that walks the street, and allow her to ply her nefarious trade unmolested, so long as she is polite and unobtrusive. As the Spartans are reputed to have said to the youth of their state, in respect to theft, " *Steal, but do not be caught at it,*" so the guardians of our public morals say, " You may be as licentious as you please, only make no public display of your immorality." The reason of this connivance at prostitution must be because our legislators and judges believe its suppression to be impossible ; and, with our system of monogamy, it is impossible. If there must be a multitude of women unmarried and unprovided for, there will be a multitude of prostitutes ; and, if there are a multitude of prostitutes, there will be a multitude of men, who, like Shakspeare's Falstaff, will decline marriage, because they can be " better accommodated than with a wife : " and so the evil will go on continually increasing and propagating itself. The Foundling Hospital, the Five Points House of Industry, and the Home for Friendless and Abandoned Women, must be built alongside of the brothel ; and their numerous inmates must be maintained either by public tax or by Christian charity (most frequently by the latter) : so that honest men must support their own wives and children and also the cast-off drabs and bastards of un-principled libertines. If we must have public prostitutes, let us have them openly and boldly, as the ancient Greeks and Romans did ; and let them be publicly licensed, as they were under Caligula, and as they are said to be still in France ; and let the state derive, at least, sufficient revenue from them to bury their murdered infants, and to bring up their abandoned foundlings.

THE HIGHER LAW OF CHRISTIAN PHILANTHROPY.

Let me not be misunderstood in what I have just said. I do not depreciate that form of charity which seeks out the victims of licentiousness, and makes them the special objects of its beneficence. I would not say one word in its disparagement. On the contrary, I acknowledge its genuineness. Such charity is worthy of great commendation : it is in a special sense true Christian charity, for it is eminently Christ-like ; since he came to seek and to save the lost, and disdained not to be called the Friend of publicans and sinners. But what I demand is this, that this form of Christian char-

ity should so expand its efforts and its aims as
fully to meet the case, and yield a permanent
and radical relief to that class of the poor and
miserable which it has taken under its charge.
Let its aims be so comprehensive, so high, so broad,
and so deep, that it cannot be satisfied with any
thing less than a prevention of the " social evil "
which it has hitherto attempted only to alleviate.
And it is certainly no slander to our present charities of this kind, to say that the alleviation which
they have effected is altogether inadequate.   The
miserable victims of this vice are increasing
faster than the ability or the disposition to relieve
them.   The most enthusiastic philanthropists have
already become disheartened in vainly endeavoring to furnish sufficient relief, and they can see no
means of prevention.   They are at their wits'-
end ; and some of them have become fully aware,
that, under our present social system, no prevention can be possible.   " While sin is in the
world," some say, " we cannot prevent men and
women from sinning : they will sin, in spite of us
and in spite of every thing ; and the world itself
is growing more and more depraved and wicked

every day. All that we can do is to show Christian mercy, and grant some present relief."

But the true Christian philanthropist does not rest satisfied in such conclusions. He knows that it is not true that the world is growing worse and worse, but that facts and statistics prove the contrary. He believes in the "good time coming," and that the world is actually growing better and better. Many causes of human misery have been discovered and removed, or greatly diminished, and he hopes that more will be. The average duration of human life is actually being prolonged. The average state of health is incontestably being improved. Christianity has not been instituted in vain. It has already accomplished wonders of mercy and grace, and its blessed work of reform is still going on. The true philanthropist, therefore, must not and will not despair. If no preventive of licentiousness has hitherto been found, and if it be impossible to find any under our present social system of marriage, we must look for it under some other system. Marriage was made for man, and not man for marriage.

IS THE " SOCIAL EVIL " PREVENTIBLE?

But perhaps some may suppose that sincere and genuine piety is a sufficient preventive of licentiousness, and that, when all the people become truly converted, and well instructed in religious knowledge, then they will be secure from this vice. I have great confidence in genuine piety, and believe that it is indeed the best antidote to all the ills that flesh is heir to ; but the difficulty is, that it is this very licentiousness which is hindering people from becoming pious. And, besides this, it is not from want of religious knowledge that people become licentious : they have already had line upon line, and precept upon precept, for many successive generations. They know that licentiousness is a sin ; and they know, that, when they fall into it, they become liable to the most fearful punishments, both in this life and in the world to come : but the tyranny of monogamy has left them no alternative ; they have no other available means of gratifying the wants of nature. Marriage is impossible to half the women, and a single marriage is inadequate to the requirements

of half the men. Pious exhortation is but idle
talk to those who are sinning from the excite-
ment of amorous desire of which there is no
possible gratification except a sinful one. If the
philanthropist who is giving them these exhorta-
tions cannot point out a lawful means of meeting
those natural wants, of what profit can his exhor-
tations be? "If a brother or a sister be naked,
and destitute of daily food, and one of you say
unto them, Depart in peace, be ye warmed and
filled; notwithstanding ye give them not those
things which are needful to the body; what doth
it profit?" It is not instruction which our "destitute and abandoned women" want; they want
marriage; they want homes of their own to
shelter them, and husbands to love them and to
provide for them. And I have already demonstrated that it is their right to have them; their
natural and unquestionable right, of which the
injustice and tyranny of monogamy has cruelly
deprived them. Society has wronged them; and
with their own peculiar, intuitive instinct they feel
it, though they cannot tell exactly how. Society,
somehow, has made war upon them, most un-

justly; and, when they become licentious, it is from an instinctive feeling of self-defence; it is only to take such justifiable revenge upon society as a state of warfare authorizes, and has, in a manner, rendered necessary.

Now, let this warfare cease. Let the women have their rights. Let every woman have a husband and a home; and let every man have as many women as he can love, and as can love him, and as he is able to support, until all the women are provided for: then, and not till then, will prostitution cease; and then the happy time that the poet dreamed of, when he put the apparently extravagant sentiment into his hero's mouth, which I have placed upon my titlepage, will have come at last, and

" There shall be no more widows in the land." *

---

* " No man who loves his kind can in these days rest content with waiting as a servant upon human misery, when it is in so many cases possible to anticipate and avert it. Prevention is better than cure; and it is now clear to all that a large part of human suffering is preventible by improved social arrangements. Charity will now, if it be genuine, fix upon this enterprise as greater, more widely and permanently beneficial,

MONOGAMY OCCASIONS SEDUCTION AND RUIN.

If any of my readers have failed to see that there is any necessary connection between mo-

---

and therefore more Christian, than the other. It will not, indeed, neglect the lower task of relieving and consoling those, who, whether through the errors and unskilful arrangements of society, or through causes not yet preventible, have actually fallen into calamity. Its compassion will be all the deeper, its relief more prompt and zealous, because it does not generally, as former generations did, recognize such calamities to be part of man's inevitable destiny. When the sick man has been visited, and every thing done which skill and assiduity can do to cure him, modern charity will go on to consider the causes of his malady, and then to inquire whether others incur the same dangers, and may be warned in time. When the starving man has been relieved, modern charity inquires whether any fault in the social system deprived him of his share of Nature's bounty, any unjust advantage taken by the strong over the weak, any rudeness or want of culture in himself, wrecking his virtue and his habits of thrift." [I continue this quotation with a reservation; applying it to the first *Roman* Christians, but doubting its truthfulness in respect to the "apostolic," Jewish Christians.]

" The first Christians were probably not so much hopeless of accomplishing great social reforms, as unripe for the conception of them. They did not easily recognize evil to be evil, and did not believe, or rather had never dreamed, that it could be cured. Habit dulls the senses, and puts the critical faculty to sleep.

nogamy and female ruin, I beg them to examine
carefully the following observations. It has been
demonstrated, in a former chapter, that monogamy
leaves a multitude of women unprotected, and unprovided with the privileges of marriage. It does

---

The fierceness and hardness of ancient manners is apparent to us;
but the ancients themselves were not shocked by sights which
were familiar to them. To us it is sickening to think of the
gladiatorial show, of the massacres common in Roman warfare,
of the infanticide practised by grave and respectable citizens,
who did not merely condemn their children to death, but often
in practice, as they well knew, to what was still worse, — a life
of prostitution and beggary. The Roman regarded a gladiatorial show as we regard a hunt; the news of the slaughter of two
hundred thousand Helvetians by Cæsar, or half a million Jews
by Titus, excited in his mind a thrill of triumph; infanticide
committed by a friend appeared to him a prudent measure of
household economy. To shake off this paralysis of the moral
sense produced by habit, to see misery to be misery, and cruelty
to be cruelty, requires not merely a strong, but a trained and
matured compassion. It was as much, probably, as the first
Christian could learn at once, to relieve the sick, the starving,
and the desolate. Only after centuries of this simple philan-
thropy could they learn to criticise the fundamental usages of
society itself, and acquire courage to pronounce that, however
deeply rooted and time honored, they were in many cases
shocking to humanity.

" Closely connected with this insensibility to the real char-

not and it cannot furnish half of them with husbands and homes of their own : hence the galling bondage of female dependence ; hence the difficulty of woman's finding her " sphere." Yet there is nothing mysterious or doubtful about what constitutes her sphere ; for it is defined by the simple term " home," — that word, above all others, so charming, and so suggestive of every excellence in the female character, and of all the sweet memories which cluster round the blessed names of mother,

---

acter of common usages is a positive unwillingness to reform them. The argument of prejudice is twofold. It is not only that what has lasted a long time must be right, but also that what has lasted a long time, right or wrong, must be intended to continue. We are advanced by eighteen hundred years beyond the apostolic generation. Our minds are set free, so that we may boldly criticise the usages around us, knowing them to be but imperfect essays toward order and happiness, and no divinely or supernaturally ordained constitution which it would be impious to change. We have witnessed improvements in physical well-being which incline us to expect further progress, and make us keen-sighted to detect the evils and miseries that remain. Thus ought the enthusiasm of humanity to work in these days, and thus, plainly enough, it does work. These investigations are constantly being made, these reforms commenced." — ECCE HOMO.

sister, and bride. But, alas! the practical mystery
with an immense number of women still remains;
and that is, how to find a home. A father's house
is no longer a home to many a young woman; perhaps that father is poor, and the burden of years
is at last superadded to that of poverty. He cheerfully toiled for his child while she was young and
necessarily dependent upon him; and, as she grew
up to womanhood, he stinted not to bestow upon
her such learning and such accomplishments as his
scanty means could command; and his heart was
often cheered by the hope of seeing her well married and well settled in life: but, as these hopes are
not realized, he begins to feel the burden of her
maintenance. "She is old enough to provide for
herself," and "Why doesn't she get married?"
Sure enough! poor thing, why doesn't she? But
oh! how cruel to reproach her with her involuntary
dependence and her miserable lot! And it is an
immense relief to her, when it is at length decided
that she must go out to service. And so she goes
to toil for bread among strangers. Her frail form
is overburdened, and often broken down, by unre-
mitting and ill-requited labor, and her young heart

not unfrequently corrupted and hardened by unavoidable contact and contamination with vice.

THE HARLOT'S PROGRESS.

What wonder is it, then, that, under such circumstances, the unprotected, wearied, homesick girl should yield a reluctant ear to the seductive flatteries of the profligate libertine, who scruples not to utter vows of constancy, and draw fond pictures of future affluence, to be shared with her ; but who, having accomplished his fiendish purpose, and stolen from her, forever, her only dower of innocence and purity, now ignores his vows and promises, and casts her off, to seek and ruin another victim ! What shall become of that poor, desolate, guilty, heart-broken wretch thus ruthlessly abandoned ? Alas ! the result is scarcely doubtful : it is too often experienced. Despised by herself no less than by the world, driven in anger from the paternal threshold, the gates of honest toil and the doors of Christian charity closed against her, she yields to hopeless despair, and, even for the miserable purpose of prolonging a wretched existence, she abandons herself at length to a life of open shame ; becoming herself the means of propagating that misery of which she is such an unhappy victim.

The artificial system of monogamy offers up other sacrifices on the unholy altar of abandoned lust, besides those furnished from among the daughters of toil or the victims of seduction. The accomplished, the refined, the proud, and the wealthy have furnished their full proportion to swell the aggregate number of the lost. We hope, of course, that much the larger portion of women who have been well brought up, and have failed to marry, have lived and died honest old maids. They never quite lost their hope. Poor, simple souls, they had always been told that their husbands would come for them by and by ; that there is a Jack for every Gill, as many men as women in the world ; and so they sat and waited, —

> "Rusticus expectat, dum defluat amnis ; at ille
> Labitur et labetur in omne volubilis ævum."

And thus the ceaseless tide of human life rolls on and on, the number of competitors among marriageable maids abates not, the number of men who are ready to marry augments not. Some, therefore, among the higher and the middling ranks of life, who ought to die old maids, according to the system of monogamy, do not so die. The very pride and spirit of accomplished women have sometimes proved their ruin. When they have discovered that real men are comparatively rare in the matrimonial market, and that there are more rakes and triflers than honest lovers in society, and that there cannot be husbands and homes provided for more than half the women, — being unable to suppress all their strong susceptibilities of love, and unwilling to surrender all their rights to its enjoyment, — they have deliberately determined to enjoy what they can without marriage; and thus to defy the scorn of men and the wrath of God.

But passion does not impel so great a number of intelligent women to self-abandonment, as a desire of self-support and a dread of being an intolerable burden to others. Under such apprehensions, many unhappy women, who had been nursed in the lap of luxury, and accustomed to every indulgence during childhood, have found, after coming of age, that as year after year passed round, and no eligible opportunity of marriage occurred, their presence at home was becoming more and more unwelcome, and their formidable bills of expenses more and more reluctantly allowed, till they have at last fled from those halls of wealth, and from an intolerable dependence on churlish relatives, to a still more wretched existence in the haunts of public vice.

How great is the injustice and oppression of the social system which makes no other provision for so many of its most beautiful and originally innocent daughters than this ! Well may the poet thus rave against the social tyranny of our system.

" Cursed be the social lies that warp us from the living truth ;
 Cursed be the social wants that sin against the strength of
  youth ;
 Cursed be the sickly forms that err from honest Nature's
  rule."   TENNYSON.

MONOGAMY CAUSES CHASTITY AND RELIGION TO BE HATED.

Monogamy being partial in its privileges, and oppressive in its prohibitions, like every other oppressive and unjust thing, provokes resentment and enmity, and cannot be thoroughly maintained and honestly observed. Human nature is constantly rebelling against it, and is persistently asserting its inherent and inalienable right to all the benefits of love and marriage, of which this system has deprived it. These struggles for freedom from the oppression of monogamy, being made in ignorance of the privileges of polygamy, have assumed the form of defiant transgression against the laws of chastity itself; for the popular conscience is so depraved by the erroneous education of our social system, as to regard the restrictions of monogamy as identical with those of religion. And, finding them too hard to be borne, instead of resorting to the just and proper alternative of polygamy, many persons have broken away from all moral restraint whatever, have given loose rein to impetuous passion, and have become lost to every sentiment of virtue and to every hope of heaven.

As Christianity itself was outraged and repudiated at the period of the French Revolution, on account of the abuses of Roman Catholicism, with which the popular mind had confounded it (Romanism being the only acknowledged form of Chris-

tianity then known in that country, so that, when
they rose against it, they rose against Christianity
itself, and became raging demons of barbarity and
crime), so now, throughout Europe and America, is
chastity outraged and religion repudiated on account of the unjust restrictions which monogamy
has instituted in their names.   But neither religion
nor chastity are the real objects of this hatred.
All men sincerely respect the one and revere the
other. Yet many cannot see how to assert their
natural rights and achieve their long-lost freedom
without destroying both.   Polygamy alone solves
the problem how those rights can be enjoyed while
chastity is preserved and religion maintained ; for
polygamy alone can honestly furnish sufficient indulgence of love to all the men, and sufficient protection of marriage to all the women.   Monogamy
says to half the women, " Ye cannot marry, and
hence ye shall not love ; " and to every man it
says, " Thou canst marry but one woman, and one
only shalt thou love," without regard to the condition of that woman, or her ability or inability to
meet his conjugal wants.

It is a physical fact that women are not only

less inclined to amorous passion than the men, at all times, but they are also subject to interruptions and periodical changes, which men do not experience. During the long period of lactation, or nursing, most women have a positive repugnance to the embraces of love, as well as during the progress of certain nervous chronic disorders peculiar to the sex, which are aggravated, if not caused, by frequent connubial intercourse ; so much so, that some medical men insist upon entire separation from the marriage-bed during the continuance of these disorders, and also during the period of lactation. At such times, one would suppose that no civilized man, or at least that no Christian man, could be so brutal and so cruel as to force his wife to yield to his propensities against her own inclinations and in spite of her repeated and earnest remonstrances : but nothing is more certain than that there are many thousands of just such Christian men ; for what can the poor monogamist do? The healthful currents of vigorous life impel him to amorous desire ; and he cannot afford to shut down the gates or to shut off the steam. To do so would involve immense loss of pleasure and of power. The passions furnish the only streams to turn the machinery of action; and love is the strongest of them all. While there is the hope of indulgence, the machinery runs smoothly, and the whole man is full of life and buoyancy and power; but, if this master-passion must be repressed, its unnatural restraint absorbs all the remaining strength of the man, and he is no better than a hermit or a monk. Hence no vigorous man is willing to endure this restraint. Yet the Christian monogamist has been taught that it is both a sin and a shame to look for the gratification of his desires away from home; so the poor heart-broken and back-broken wife must submit to torture, and so the otherwise kind and honorable husband must commit violence upon his dearest friend, whom he has most solemnly promised to love and to cherish, in sickness and in health, till death shall part them. Many a poor wife then prays for death to part them soon. But other men, at such times, disdaining to avail themselves of extorted pleasures, which can afford so little satisfaction, and despising that religion which will justify or allow such cruel brutality, then steal away from their unwilling

wives, and, in defiance of the most solemn obligations and sacred laws of God and man, go and do
worse; defiling the beds of virgin innocence, or
wasting their health and strength upon vile prostitutes. Which horn of this trilemma should the
vigorous husband of this invalid woman choose;
imbecile continence, wicked licentiousness, or matrimonial brutality? Would not polygamy be an alternative preferable to either? would it not be more
just and more merciful than either? It is just and
merciful to both the men and the women; it pre-
serves the marriage-bed undefiled; it provides husbands for all the women; and it allows each man
to take more than one wife when circumstances
warrant and require it. And they often do require
it. The extraordinary vehemence and intensity of
the amorous propensity which some men experience is sufficient of itself to require it. Such
men can no more restrain this desire than that for
their necessary food. They may call to their assistance every motive to continence that can be
drawn from heaven and earth and hell, but they
often call in vain; for the intensity of this passion
sweeps down every barrier, and rushes to its grati-

fication. If, then, there will be and there must be
indulgence, let it be such as is regulated and con-
trolled by divine and natural law. God who made
man, and who knows what is in man, has provided
sufficient means to supply his natural amorous
wants. Marriage is that means ; and, as one wife
is not always sufficient, he has provided more.
There are women enough, and no man need be
either pining or sinning for the want of them.

> " Take the good the gods provide thee :
>   Lovely Thais sits beside thee,
>   Blooming like an Eastern bride,
>   In flower of youth and beauty's pride.
>   Happy, happy, happy pair !
>   None but the brave,
>   None but the brave,
>   None but the brave deserves the fair."

GREAT MEN ARE ALWAYS POLYGAMISTS.

And it is the brave, the gifted, the talented, that
deserve the fair, who have always desired the fair,
and won the fair. " Lovely Thais " never refuses
to unveil her charms to the true hero. Great men
always recognize the voice of God in the voice of

Nature, no matter under what social system they may live. They yield to the natural and the divine behests, even though they transgress the laws of ordinary social life. They obey God rather than men ; and this obedience is the first element of their greatness. Ordinary laws may be sufficient to restrain ordinary men ; but when a Samson is within their bonds, those bonds are snapped asunder like the green withes and the new ropes of Delilah. Yet, were not our social laws so manifestly arbitrary and oppressive, such eminent philosophers as Plato, Aristotle, and Bacon, such noble heroes as Alexander, Cæsar, Napoleon, and Nelson, such divine poets as Goethe, Burns, and Byron, and such enlightened statesmen as Pericles, Augustus, Buckingham, Palmerston, and Webster, and many thousands more, would never have incurred the odium of libertinism as they have. Although they lived under the system of monogamy, they would not and did not submit to it. Their noble natures required a larger indulgence, and they took it, law or no law, like brave men as they were. And there are many more such men than the world dreams of in its narrow monogamic philosophy ;

and yet it is a shame and a pity that our social laws
cannot be so amended, and brought into harmony
with those of God and Nature, that our noblest
men would yield them the most prompt obedience.
And is it not a sad pity, a burning shame, and a
fearful wrong that our laws are such, that such men
cannot acknowledge their mistresses, and avow
their children? The wrongs of these women and
children are crying to God from the ground, and
he will hear and judge. These great men are
brave; but they are not brave enough. They have
no just right to practise their polygamy in the
dark. Let us have either an honest monogamy or
an avowed polygamy. Hence it is that I am called
by the justice of God and the sufferings of humanity to appeal to every honorable sentiment in mankind in behalf of a greater freedom to marry, and
a greater purity of the marriage relation. Let
us have such marriage laws, that whatever relations any honorable man shall determine to form
with the other sex can be honorably formed and
honorably maintained.

HYPOCRISY OF MONOGAMY.

But an honest monogamy is an impossibility.
Wherever it is practised, it is a system of hypocrisy.
It is a veil of abstemiousness assumed to conceal a
mass of hidden corruption. Its direct tendency is
to stimulate the contemptible vices of intrigue and
lying, as well as the equally detestable ones of prostitution and adultery. By attempting to deprive
one-half the women of any lawful and honorable
means of amorous pleasure, and by allowing the
men only partial and inadequate means, it impels
a multitude of each sex to secret transgression, or
else to open profligacy ; and thus the laws of chastity are violated on every hand, and truthfulness,
integrity, purity, and honor are becoming but un-
meaning terms.

No one familiar with social life in Europe will
dare to dispute that a large proportion of the
upper classes of society there are addicted to some
form of licentiousness. It is often observed there,
that, as soon as the women marry, they throw off
the restraints of chastity, and encourage secret
lovers ; and while each of the men live openly with

one woman only, or with none, yet they indulge in promiscuous criminal intercourse to an incredible extent.   Now, which social system is the more honorable and manly, the more virtuous and pure, the one more in accordance with Nature and the laws of Nature's God, — a pretended and a corrupt monogamy, or an open and honest polygamy? Which manifests the more base and selfish passion, — the man who espouses the partners of his love, and takes them to his home and his heart, and provides for them and their children, or the man who steals away from his house in the dark, and indulges his dishonorable and degrading passion in secret places, and then abandons the partners of his guilty pleasure to a life of wretchedness and shame and want?

> "Domestic happiness, thou only bliss
> Of Paradise that has survived the fall!
> Though few now taste thee unimpaired and pure,
> Or, tasting, long enjoy thee !   .   .   .
> Thou art the nurse of Virtue : in thine arms
> She smiles, appearing, as in truth she is,
> Heaven-born, and destined to the skies again.
> Thou art not known where Pleasure is adored,
> That reeling goddess with the zoneless waist

And wandering eyes, still leaning on the arm
Of Novelty, her fickle, frail support;
For thou art meek and constant, hating change,
And finding in the calm of truth-tried love
Joys that her stormy raptures never yield.
Forsaking thee, what shipwreck have we made
Of honor, dignity, and fair renown!
Till prostitution elbows us aside
In all our crowded streets; and senates seem
Convened for purposes of empire less
Than to release the adulteress from her bond."

                       THE TASK.

CHAPTER VIII.

THE NECESSARY RELATION OF MONOGAMY TO IMMORALITY AND CRIME.

MARRIAGE PREVENTS CRIME.

It is an acknowledged fact that crime is much more prevalent among unmarried persons than among the married ; for the married man's family becomes a pledge to society for his good behavior : nor can the married woman disgrace herself without disgracing also her husband and her children. That system, therefore, which provides marriage for the greater number must be the more favorable to the promotion of public virtue and morality. It has already been demonstrated that polygamy provides for the marriage of the greater number of the women than monogamy can ; and it will not be difficult to prove that it also conduces to the marriage of the greater number of the men : for there are always a great many men

who will not marry, so long as they can obtain
the gratification of their propensities without marriage, which they can do as long as there are so
many unmarried women as there must be where-
ever monogamy prevails. The more rich and
luxurious monogamous society becomes, the more
abandoned women there will be, and the fewer
marriages and the more crime. But let the system of polygamy be adopted, and then all the
women will be wanted for wives; and, as they
can then obtain husbands and homes of their own,
but few will prefer to follow a loose and vicious
course of life. And then the men, being deprived
of the opportunity of illicit indulgence, will be
compelled to marry; and their marriage will refine
and humanize them, and preserve them from
many of those vices and immoralities to which
they are now addicted. There are many crimes
against which the moral sentiment of humanity
revolts, but which are constantly forced upon mankind by the tyranny of monogamy, and which
nothing but a return to the purer system of
polygamy can restrain and prevent. Among
many of these crimes and moral evils caused or

aggravated by monogamy, and which would be greatly diminished by polygamy, I can mention only a few.

The violation of the marriage-vow constitutes the crime of adultery, — a crime which has always been regarded with the greatest detestation among mankind, and which, in ancient times, was punished with death. The definition of adultery, like that of marriage, depends upon the social system which we adopt. According to the system of monogamy, if any married person has sexual intercourse with any one, except his own wife, or her own husband, then he or she is guilty of adultery; but if the other party to the same act be unmarried, then that unmarried person is not guilty of adultery, but of fornication only. That is, if a married man has intercourse with another man's wife, then both are guilty of adultery; but if an unmarried man has intercourse with a married woman, then she is guilty of adultery, but he is not. According to the system of polygamy, if any man has intercourse with another man's wife, they are both guilty of adultery; but if any man has intercourse with an unmarried woman, then both are guilty of fornication. That is, it is the married or unmarried state of the woman, and not of the man, that determines the nature of the crime; and both parties to the same act are always by this system held guilty of the same offence. A careful examination of the laws of God and of Nature will enable us to determine which of these definitions is correct, and will also assist us in the determination of the more important question, Which social system is right?

1. If a married woman admit any other man to her bed except her husband, her offspring becomes spurious, or at least uncertain, and her husband may have another man's child imposed upon him instead of his own, to be supported, and to inherit his estate; but no such uncertainty occurs from the intercourse of one man with several women.

2. If a wife admit the embrace of another lover, it always implies an alienation of her affections from her husband: but it does not imply an alienation of her husband's affections to take another woman, for his first wife is not always

capable of fulfilling his conjugal desires ; and it is sometimes as much out of regard to her health and comfort as to his own gratification, that he is impelled to take another.

3. If a woman is having intercourse with several men at the same time, she is living in uncleanness, and in constant liability of inducing within herself, and communicating to all her lovers, the most loathsome and incurable diseases ; her mind and heart become hopelessly depraved, and she incurs the utter loss of all self-respect and all public estimation : but no such diseases of body or degradation of character attach to the man who is living with several women.

These natural laws are fully ratified and confirmed by the divine law : " The man that committeth adultery with another man's wife, the adulterer and the adulteress shall surely be put to death." " But if a man entice a maid that is not betrothed, and lie with her, he shall surely endow her to be his wife." " Because he hath humbled her, he may not put her away all his life." " And Nathan said to David, Thou art the man. Thus saith the Lord, I delivered thee out of the hand of

Saul, and I gave thee thy master's house and thy master's wives into thy bosom; and gave thee the house of Israel and of Judah, and if that had been too little, I would moreover have given thee such and such things. Wherefore hast thou despised the commandment of the Lord to do evil in his sight, and hast taken the wife of Uriah the Hittite to be thy wife? Now, therefore, the sword shall never depart from thy house, because thou hast despised me, and hast taken the wife of Uriah the Hittite to be thy wife." * It seems unnecessary to cite further proofs. The entire Bible confirms the definition of adultery as given by the system of polygamy.

The civil laws of those States practising monogamy, in defining adultery, are full of contradictions and obscurities. Their theory requires that all married persons, both men and women, who have intercourse with any others except their own husbands or their own wives, should be called adulterers, and considered equally criminal; but with an open Bible before them, and living Nature

---

* Ex. xxii. 16; Lev. xx. 10; Deut. xxii. 22–29; 2 Sam. xii. 7–10.

all around them, they approach, sometimes, very
near to the distinctions set forth in polygamy.
The following is Dr. Noah Webster's definition:
"*Adultery.* Violation of the marriage-bed; a crime
or civil injury which introduces, or may introduce,
into a family, a spurious offspring. In *common
usage*, adultery means the unfaithfulness of any
married person to the marriage-bed. *By the laws
of Connecticut*, the sexual intercourse of any man
with a married woman is the *crime* of adultery in
both; such intercourse of a married man with an
unmarried woman is fornication in both, and
adultery of the man, within the meaning of the
law respecting divorce; but not a felonious
adultery in either, or the crime of adultery at
common law, or by the statute. This latter
offence is, in England, proceeded with only in the
ecclesiastical courts."

This definition, according to the laws of Connecticut, is the very one which polygamy requires,
with the exception of that part of it relating to
divorce; and doubtless the God-fearing legislators
of the "Land of Steady Habits" who framed this
statute were more familiar with the Bible than

with Roman codes, and, besides, had very little respect for the authority of popes or councils. In Massachusetts, also, the statute requires that "when the crime is committed between a married woman and a man who is unmarried, the man shall be deemed guilty of adultery." *Rev. Stat. of Mass.*, 1860. In most of the States of the American Union, however, the laws define adultery, according to common usage, as the theory of monogamy requires. And the consequence is, that it is regarded as a very trifling crime by the statutes of those States; the common penalty being only one hundred dollars' fine, or six months' imprisonment, even this light penalty being rarely inflicted; for the public conscience is so depraved by the false definitions of monogamous jurisprudence in respect to this crime, that few men will prosecute and few juries will convict either an adulterer or an adulteress.

> " The adulteress! what a theme for angry verse !
> What provocation to the indignant heart
> That feels for injured love !   But I disdain
> The nauseous task to paint her as she is, —

Cruel, abandoned, glorying in her shame !
No : let her pass, and, charioted along
In guilty splendor, shake the public ways :
The frequency of crimes has washed them white."

MURDER.

It is a notorious fact, that, where the system of monogamy prevails, the most common cause of murder is unhappy marriages. Husbands murder their wives, and wives murder their husbands, or incite others to do it, almost every week. When love turns to hatred, it is the bitterest kind of hatred; and when people hate each other, their hatred becomes the more intense, the more closely they are bound together. The bonds of matrimony are softer than silk, and sweeter than wreaths of flowers, so long as mutual love and mutual confidence subsist; but when these are banished from the domestic altar, and their places usurped by distrust and jealousy, then those bonds become heavier than iron shackles, and more corroding than fetters of brass. Under such circumstances, a separation of some kind is eagerly desired. This desire is spontaneous and instinctive; but **the** marriage-vow has been so solemnly uttered and recorded, that there can be no honorable separation but death. Then the dreadful crime of murder is conceived and cherished and pondered in the mind, until it takes complete possession of it. The idea of murder is begotten between the desire of dissolving the marriage and the desire of maintaining one's public honor. And both desires cannot be gratified in any other way. Divorce is dishonorable. It occasions endless talk and scandal, and divulges family secrets. It makes one inevitably notorious. It often involves immense expense. Persons, therefore, whose desires are naturally impetuous, and who are determined to obtain a speedy separation from their hated husbands or wives, are peculiarly liable to this crime. They study out a plan that promises complete success. They are quite sure that they can manage to murder their companions without being found out. At all events, they often do murder them, and run the risk of being found out, as well as the additional risk of divine punishment in the world to come. Many cases of murder for this cause never are found out; but enough are discovered to prove that the dreadful crime is one of frequent occurrence. It has been brought to light that some men have murdered a number of wives, and some women a number of husbands in succession. The nursery story of Bluebeard may be a horrible fiction ; but it is a fiction founded on fact: there must be some verisimilitude about it, or it could never have interested so many generations as it has. Many well-authenticated instances of wife-murder have occurred for which no excuse of jealousy or domestic infelicity can be urged, and which can only be accounted for on the ground of men's capricious desires and love of change. The history of Henry VIII., king of England, and his six wives, most of whom were successively murdered to make room for their successors, is an obvious and an authentic instance.

Now, polygamy furnishes the only sufficient preventive of this horrible crime ; for almost any man would sooner support an extra wife, if the usages of society would allow it, than to take the life of his present wife, at the imminent risk of his own. And many men will do it, and are now doing it, even against the usages of society, and in spite of the regulations of monogamy. Thus King Henry

II., less sanguinary, or more independent of public opinion, than his brilliant descendant above mentioned, still permitted his queen Eleanor to live, and to wear the crown, though he often preferred the society of the fair Rosamond to hers, and often repaired to her sylvan bowers at Woodstock to enjoy it. And most of the sovereigns of Europe have followed his example; but, like Charles II. and the four Georges, they keep their mistresses nearer court than at Woodstock.

DIVORCE.

The marriage-relation is designed to be a permanent and an inseparable one. The parties take each other by the hand, and mutually plight their troth, for better or for worse, to love and to cherish, in prosperity and in adversity, in health and in sickness, till death shall part them. Such a union is most honorable : it is most admirable. But, under the system of monogamy, it is often impracticable. Although the laws of Christ allow of but one cause for divorce, — the unfaithfulness of the wife to the marriage-vow, — and although every State that practises monogamy claims to be a Christian State, yet civil laws allow of divorce for the most trifling causes. The excuse is made, that, when married persons are unhappy in their marriage-relation, divorce alone can prevent neglect and abuse ; and it may prevent murder. So they allow them to commit one great crime to prevent their committing another and a greater. This is, of course, fallacious reasoning. But, if it were most exact reasoning, the remedy is dangerous, unnecessary, and directly at variance with the laws of God. Polygamy is a safer and a surer remedy or rather preventive of both divorce and murder than any violation of divine law can be. The laws of God and of Nature always harmonize with each other ; and the only manner in which we can perfect our civil laws is to bring them into perfect accordance with the former.

Most men who desire a divorce would prefer polygamy, if it were practicable and lawful. A man does not often undertake to repudiate his present wife, until he begins to desire another. And that other one is already selected and already loved ; but the love cannot be consummated. And nothing but the desire of consummating this love carries him through with the divorce. For, if the law of the land favors the divorce, there still remains the law of God to oppose it; and hence divorces are usually difficult, expensive, annoying, and slow. It took Henry VIII. five years, with all his wealth and power, to divorce himself from his first wife, Catharine of Aragon, in favor of Anne Boleyn, with whom he was desperately in love all the while. If she had yielded to his solicitations, and granted him illicit gratification, it is not at all probable that he would ever have prosecuted the divorce to its termination. And thus is every divorce more or less tedious, and it ought to be. Christianity forbids it, the wife resists it, children plead, and friends expostulate against it, the world wonders and stares; and yet, in spite of all opposition, the vehement passions of men often drive them through it. Yet the greatest suffering of all is that of the man's own conscience, who persists in it. To do such violence to the most solemn laws of God and the most honorable sentiments of mankind is no light crime, whatever the laws of the State may term it. Polygamy furnishes the only preventive of this great social evil.

If a man loves another woman, and is resolved to have her, let him take her, and keep her, and keep his first one also. Napoleon Bonaparte never would have divorced Josephine, had polygamy been deemed lawful and proper. Yet no man ever had a fairer pretext for divorce upon any mere prudential considerations than he had. Her virtue was unquestionable. It was not only above reproach, it was above suspicion. But all hopes of her having offspring had failed. His desire for an heir was most intense, most natural, and most commendable. It seemed to be all that was wanting to secure the stability of his throne, the good of his people, and the peace of the world. Yet, according to the system of monogamy, the only manner in which these very desirable ends could be attained was by the divorce of Josephine, by whose alliance he had been brought to more public notice, and been greatly assisted in his successful career, and who was one of the loveliest and noblest women that ever wore a crown. The divorce was consummated, the reasons for it were publicly announced; but the moral sense of the world was shocked, and Napoleon was at once pronounced a tyrant and a monster. And this act is still held by many to be the turning-point both in his personal character and in his public career. Before this, all his history is bright; after it, all is dark. One cannot, even now, after so long a time, contemplate the tears of Josephine and the subsequent disasters of Napoleon, without cursing the narrow bigotry of monogamy, and wishing that the golden age of polygamy had returned before his day.

At the court of David, King of Israel, even the rape and the incest of Tamar were not so unpardonable as her abandonment. Although shocked and indignant at the brutal violence of her half-brother Amnon, yet her tenderness could not deny some pity to the intensity of his passion. "Nay, my brother, do not force me," she said. "Speak to the king; for he will not withhold me from thee." But when his lust had been sated, and he commanded her to be gone, she refused to go; saying, "This evil in sending me away is greater than the other." * Then he caused her to be put out forcibly, and the door to be bolted. It was this insulting divorce added to her forcible humilia-

---

* 2 Sam. xiii.

tion that broke her heart. The latter she might forgive, the former she could not ; and she rent her purple robes, and went out crying with her hand upon her head. It was this cruel repudiation that whetted the dagger of Absalom to avenge her wrongs, and it was this that fills up the measure of Amnon's guilt in the judgment of every honest heart. God did not require David to put away Bathsheba after he had once ravished her, and would not have permitted him to do so, had he desired it, although he had obtained her by blood and fraud. His punishment must come in some other manner. Their marriage, once consummated by cohabitation, was complete and indissoluble. How differently would a similar case be now decided by the ecclesiastical courts of modern Europe ! Can men's judgment be more just than God's?

PROCURING ABORTION.

The murder of the child *in embryo* is a crime prohibited by law, and most repugnant to humanity. Yet it is one which the system of monogamy is obliged to wink at and tolerate. This horrid crime is becoming more and more common every year, till it is now somewhat fashionable, especially as it is more commonly practised by fashionable people. Not many years ago, the person who dispensed drugs for such vile purposes was branded as a villain, or looked upon as a hateful hag; a Locusta, whose fit dwelling-place was some dark cave among volcanic mountains, and whose fit companions were venomous serpents and wild foxes : but it is now currently reported that one of the popular compounders of these death-dealing drugs is deemed worthy of the honor of knighthood,* and is appointed physician extraordinary to the queen. Almost every newspaper now contains a well-displayed advertisement, addressed " to the ladies," setting forth the powerful properties of some specific for " removing obstructions," and " bringing on the monthly periods," with entire certainty; and although these drugs will be " sure to cause miscarriage," yet they are at the same time so " mild and safe as not to be injurious to the most delicate constitution." Such are some of the most impudent

---

* Sir (?) James Clarke.

claims of the modern abortionist. But I cannot go on.

For full details I beg to refer my readers to the public journals of the day.

But the manufacturers and the consumers of drugs for these abominable practices are not the only ones responsible for the crime. Monogamy is responsible for it. The entire social system is corrupt. The most respectable merchants and apothecaries deal in these drugs, the most respectable journals advertise them, everybody reads about them; yet no protesting voice is raised, either against the use of them or the traffic in them. The ministers of religion, the proper censors of the public morals, are silent: the subject is too indelicate for them to allude to. The police-magistrates and other officers of the law make no effort to bring the guilty parties to justice, except in the most shocking and notorious instances, where the life of the mother is taken, as well as that of the child.

Intelligent and respectable physicians, who have the best opportunities of knowing, state that this vice is now practised more commonly by married women than by the unmarried; and it is not difficult to account for it. Under the system of monogamy, the wife attempts too much, and physical impossibilities are expected and required of her. She alone undertakes to supply all her husband's conjugal wants, and to gratify all his amorous desires; and she is quite conscious that even in the bloom of her youth, in perfect health, and in the height of her charms, she is scarcely capable of doing it: and she dreads to have any thing happen to her to make her less capable. Especially if she has already borne one child, and has passed through the long period of lactation, she remembers its effect upon herself and upon her husband with alarm. She fancies herself in danger of losing her hold upon his affections, which she wishes to retain, of course, as long as possible. She therefore takes drugs to prevent fruitfulness, and to preserve her form and beauty, in order to prevent her husband's affections being lavished upon others.

And if the system of monogamy be right, then this motive is commendable, and the reasoning based upon it is entirely valid. No wife can be blamed for wishing to prevent her husband from forming illicit attachments, and thus bringing dishonor upon himself and all his house; and the only means at her command for preventing it is to concentrate all his affections upon herself.

But polygamy is capable of suppressing this vice, or, at least, of greatly diminishing it, by removing its most powerful motives. Under the system of polygamy, the burdens as well as the privileges of the women are more equally distributed. No woman is required or expected to be always prepared for her husband's embraces, nor does she claim any more than she is able to receive, or than he is voluntarily inclined to bestow. If she is full of life, and in vigorous health, and is capable of fulfilling her conjugal duties alone, it is well: her husband is a happy man. But, if she is not able, it is still well. Her husband need not be unhappy; for he can espouse another, without reproach to her or dishonor to himself.

FECUNDITY OUGHT TO BE PROMOTED, NOT
DESTROYED.

The laws of God and of Nature concur in
bearing unqualified testimony to the desirableness
of offspring. It is the proper fruit of marriage,
of which love is the blossom. The blossom
yields a delicious but an evanescent pleasure;
but the fruit, after diligent culture and careful
preservation, is a source of perpetual delight and
honor. " Be fruitful, and multiply, and replenish
the earth and subdue it," constitutes the most important part of the divine blessing pronounced
upon the first married couple, — a benediction repeated, in substance, upon the occasion of every
subsequent marriage the particulars of which are
recorded in the Holy Bible. When the parents of
Rebecca sent her away to become the wife of
Isaac, they blessed her, and said, " Be thou the
mother of thousands of millions ; " and when
Boaz espoused Ruth the Moabitess, the people that
were in the gate, and the elders, said, " The Lord
make the woman that is come into thy house, like
Rachel and Leah, which two did build the house

of Israel." " Lo, children are a heritage of the Lord, and the fruit of the womb is his reward. As arrows are in the hand of a mighty man, so are the children of the youth. Happy is the man that hath his quiver full of them." " Thy wife shall be as a fruitful vine by the sides of thy house, thy children like olive-plants round about thy table. Behold that thus shall the man be blessed that feareth the Lord." *

As fruitfulness, on the one hand, is always declared to be a blessing, in the Bible, so barrenness, on the other hand, is declared to be a curse. The most affecting and the most memorable prayers of females recorded therein are those which beg for offspring ; and the most grateful thanksgivings are those for children borne by them. But the unnatural and unholy system of monogamy which now prevails has so strangely perverted our desires, that it seems to change the divine blessing into a curse, and the curse into a blessing. If women would now dare to pray for what they wish, they would pray for barrenness, instead of fruitfulness. Now, there must be something radically wrong in

---

* Ps. cxxvii., cxxviii.

a social system which thus presumes to reverse the course of Nature, and to contradict the divine assurances of blessing and of cursing ; and which has so fatally and deeply poisoned the mysterious springs of life, and polluted the most inviolable sanctuaries of female purity and maternal love.

> " Our Maker bids increase : who bids abstain,
>   But our destroyer, foe to God and man ? "

I doubt whether there can be any form of licentiousness more abhorrent to the laws of God and of Nature than this "Murder of the Innocents." Even fornication cannot be so great a sin. The unmarried woman who has a child in the natural way, and who bestows upon it a mother's love and a mother's care, cannot thereby become so guilty as the married woman who wilfully destroys her offspring, or who prevents her fruitfulness. There is great danger lest the general smattering of medical knowledge among us may do more harm than good. There is, alas ! a positive certainty that presumptuous quacks, who know only enough of Nature to have lost their reverence for her laws, are leading many of our honorable women astray, and are poisoning the best blood in our land. These women, like our common mother Eve, from unholy and intensely selfish motives, prompted and countenanced by our system of monogamy, are plucking the fruit of the tree of knowledge of good and evil, and intermeddling with those functions of Nature which ought to be let alone. No honorable physician, who is master of his profession, will degrade that profession so much as to descend to such vile practice. His business is not to destroy life, but to save it. He, at least, has learned the most profound respect for the laws of our being.

> " A little learning is a dangerous thing ;
>   Drink deep, or taste not the Pierian Spring.
>   There shallow draughts intoxicate the brain ;
>   But drinking largely sobers us again."

We had better know nothing of the laws of gestation than to know only enough to evade or violate them ; for they cannot be violated with impunity. The time will come when the young wife who now destroys her unborn offspring, or who otherwise wilfully and wickedly tampers with her reproductive powers, will surely mourn their loss, and will mourn as one that cannot be comforted. Like Rachel, she will beg and pray for fruitfulness, and say, " Oh ! give me children, or else I die ; " but, not like Rachel, she will beg and pray in vain. Those delicate organs once weakened by violent or unnatural means rarely regain their normal condition, and one voluntary abortion may be followed by many involuntary miscarriages. She loses all, and she is guilty of all ; and some day she will surely feel both her loss and her guilt, till it becomes, like the punishment of the first murderer, a burden too heavy to be borne. Never can she know by blissful experience the sweetness of a mother's love ; that pure and fond and tender and changeless affection, which so inspires and ennobles the female character. Never can she become quite free from the jealous suspicions of her husband, who, against his will and all his better judgment, is a perpetual prey to the green-eyed demon. Never can the spacious halls and gloomy apartments of their solitary home resound with the innocent glee of their children's voices ; no baby in the cradle ; no " daughter singing in the village choir " or the Sunday-school concert ; no son to graduate from school or college, or to inherit and transmit to future generations the family name and wealth and honors.

This is no fancy sketch nor far-fetched representation, but is a faithful protraiture of many of our New-England families. The curse of God is already upon us, and our native population is even now giving way to the more prolific races of English, Celts, and Germans. God gives the land to those who obey his marriage-laws to " be fruitful, and multiply and replenish the earth, and subdue it." As the Israelites drove out the ancient Canaanites who made their children pass through to Moloch, and as they took possession of their fruitful fields and vineyards, already planted, and of their towns and cities, already built; so these poorer, more natural and less artificial immigrants are dispossessing us. I quote once more from the Massachusetts Registration Report for 1866, page 18.

BIRTH-RATE IN MASSACHUSETTS.

" In England, during the twenty-six years 1838–1863, with a population of about eighteen millions, the average birth-rate was 3.33 per cent. In

Massachusetts, it has never been so high. In the seven years 1852–1858, it was 2.90. In the five years immediately preceding the war, 1856–1860, it was 2.85. During the four years of war, 1862–1865, the birth-rate was 2.46. We find it now rising, not to the old standard of 2.85 or 2.90, but to 2.69."

Page 28 reads as follows, —

" The foreign-born population of Massachusetts, by the census of 1865, was 265,486, the American population 999,976, and the population of unknown nativity 1,569. The last it is not easy to divide ; it seems nearer the probable truth to divide them equally. We have, then, 1,000,761 Americans, and 266,270 foreigners. And they produced in 1866, — the Americans 16,555 children, the foreigners 17,530 children ; that is to say, a child was born to every $60\frac{45}{100}$ Americans, and to every $15\frac{19}{100}$ foreigners ; the latter class being four times as productive as the former."

The birth-rate, therefore, of the Americans of Massachusetts for the year 1866 was only 1.65 per cent ; while that of the foreign population was 6.59 per cent. At this rate, not many generations will be required for them to dispossess us.

But it is unnecessary to the satisfactory analysis and comparison of the two marriage-systems to go on, to any greater length, with this painful dissection of vice, or to array any further statistical proofs in confirmation of the inherent licentiousness of monogamy. It would be easy to show that the galling bondage of restricted marriage has had, and is now having, a similar effect upon the great social evils of insanity, suicide, and self-pollution, which it has upon those other forms of vice which have been analyzed above, and to prove that polygamy would tend to mitigate them also. If these hints of mine are seized upon and properly developed by some more capable writer, and so clearly and happily set forth as to lead to a practical reform, it will be honor enough for me to have indicated its necessity and demonstrated its possibility.

CHAPTER IX.

OBJECTIONS TO POLYGAMY ANSWERED.

A FEW pages will now be devoted to a consideration of the objections which have been urged against the system of polygamy. And it may be proper to say, that if there should be any objections to it which are not here answered to every one's satisfaction, yet the superiority of this system is still maintained and proven, as long as the previous demonstrations remain valid; the objections to the contrary notwithstanding. It is often the case that a proposition may be true, and at the same time it may not be possible to answer all the objections to it. There are unanswerable objections to a democratic or popular form of government; and yet for some nations, such a form of government may, on the whole, be the best one.

DOES POLYGAMY CAUSE JEALOUSY?

It has been objected that polygamy cannot be reasonable or right, since it causes jealousy among the different women in the same family. But it cannot be proved that jealousy is confined to any particular social system: it is, unfortunately, too common to every system. It is inherent in human nature, and must be regarded as one of its inseparable infirmities. Yet, so far from being most violent under the system of polygamy, the opposite is the fact; for it is always most violent when secret intrigue is carried on, and when the dreaded rival does not sustain an open and an acknowledged relation to the husband, but when the tenderness between him and that rival, whether real or suspected, is only secretly indulged: so that monogamy really furnishes more occasion for the exercise of this cruel passion than polygamy. In the latter system, the claims of the different women are acknowledged and understood; the parties all stand in well-defined relations to each other, and violent jealousy, under such circumstances, must be comparatively rare.

IS POLYGAMY DEGRADING TO WOMEN?

It has also been objected, that polygamy cannot be reasonable and right, since it places men and women on terms of social inequality; it exalts man, and degrades woman; it makes her dependent on his will; it demands of her her undivided love and fidelity towards him, while he is permitted to lavish his affections upon as many as he may please. But all this is not degrading to her. It is the only thing that saves her from degradation. The experience of every age and of every community has proved that many men cannot and will not content themselves with one woman. There must be polygamy, or else there must be prostitution; and prostitution is wickedness, and wickedness is degradation.

Nor is there any thing degrading in woman's dependence upon man. This dependence is natural, and honorable to her. It is the very position which she herself voluntarily and instinctively assumes towards him. The entire code of polite, social intercourse between the two sexes is founded on this principle of her nature. Not only in

14

times of real danger, but at all times, she loves to lean upon the strong, brave arm of man, and willingly confesses her own timidity and weakness. And these qualities are so far from degrading her, that they only render her the more attractive and lovely. The manly gallant is as ready to afford assistance as she is to accept it. In riding, in walking, in dancing, in sailing, in bathing, in the public assembly, in the social gathering, and everywhere where it is possible to receive attention and accept assistance and protection, it is equally pleasing and ennobling for her to receive, and for him to bestow them.

WOMAN'S RIGHTS.

They are her rights, — her woman's rights. I believe in woman's rights, and I believe that polygamy is the system that can best assure them to her ; for, as it is a mathematical certainty that there are more women than men in the world, some men must assume the protection of more than one woman each, or some women must be deprived of their rights. The most sacred and the most precious of all her rights are her rights to a husband and a home; and it is no more a degradation to her to share that home and that husband with another woman than it is to share other benefits and other attentions from the same man, in common with other women. No woman considers herself degraded to walk abroad with her hand upon a man's arm while another woman has her hand upon the other arm; thus they often appear in public, at balls and concerts and lectures and churches. For the time being, they are both willingly dependent upon his protection and his bounty; and he is also dependent upon each of them for the benefits of their companionship and the charms of their society. He could not so fully enjoy those entertainments without them. For example, there are two female friends residing together, and mutually dependent upon each other for many of their social enjoyments, and for much of their intellectual and moral culture. A worthy young man of their acquaintance calls upon them frequently, and admires them both; and they enjoy his visits, for neither of them have any other male associate. At length he invites them both to a public entertainment. Neither of them would be willing to leave her friend, and go with him alone; nor could he well endure the thought of enjoying himself abroad with one, while the other would be deserted and neglected at home, — the other who would enjoy the entertainment so much, and whose enjoyment would so much enhance theirs. Now, if this triple companionship shall ripen into friendship, and the friendship into love, and the love shall result in a triple marriage, where is the degradation? Would it not be still more heartless to desert either of the friends now, when each heart is thrilling with the harmonious music of the triple love? Let the words of divine wisdom answer, —

"Two are better than one, . . . and a threefold cord is not quickly broken."

There is a want in the female nature which impels her to seek and to appreciate the society of a male friend, which no number of associates of her own sex can fully satisfy. I have stood by the gates of the cotton-mill, and seen the multitudes of female operatives stream out of an evening, and I marked their lonesome appearance as they repaired to their respective homes. Homes, did I say? Ah! any thing but homes, — their boarding-houses. There I have seen them sit down, by scores, to the dinner-table, and eat their dinners in the utmost silence, as if each one was entirely isolated from all social and agreeable companionship. Oh, what loneliness! how hard! how bitter! Yet many of them were radiant with the charms of womanhood, and each one capable of adorning and blessing a home, but which few of them will ever enjoy; for they are not only the unwilling victims of poverty and toil, but the willing votaries of fashion, and the unconscious slaves of monogamy.

MASCULINE POWER AND FEMININE COMPLAISANCE.

Those qualities of mind and person which impel a woman to seek the protection of the stronger sex, arising from her natural weakness and timidity, are really those very qualities which inspire the deepest admiration; yet, should a man happen to display these feminine qualities, they only render him supremely contemptible. A man must be strong, self-reliant, and courageous. No woman can devotedly love a man, unless she sees, or thinks she sees, in him a *power* of mind or of body, or of both, which Nature has denied to her. It is this power which she intuitively admires and venerates and worships, even though its exercise over her may be arbitrary and tyrannical. The Sabine matrons loved their Roman lords none the less because they had seized them with the strong hand; and a woman is always and everywhere more ready to forgive the too great ardor and boldness of a lover than his unmanly timidity and shame. For a wife to look up to her husband for authority and guidance is as natural as to look to him for protection from danger; and this is as natural as breathing. It is therefore true, though it may seem hard to some to admit it, that it is his right and duty to exercise authority, and her right and privilege to practise complaisance and submission.

> "Whence true authority in man; though both
> Not equal, as their sex not equal seemed;
> For contemplation he, and valor formed;
> For softness she, and sweet attractive grace;
> He for God only, she for God in him.
> His fair large front and eye sublime declared
> Absolute rule; and hyacinthine locks

Round from his parted forelock manly hung
Clustering, but not beneath his shoulders broad;
She, as a veil, down to the slender waist
Her unadorned golden tresses wore,
Dishevelled, but in wanton ringlets waved,
As the vine curls her tendrils, which implied
Subjection, but required with gentle sway," &c.

PARADISE LOST, Book iv.

Yet while God and Nature have constituted man the superior to woman in strength and courage and authority, these principles do not render her relation to man one of degradation or even of general inferiority; for there are many other and no less admirable qualities in which she surpasses him. Her moral and religious sentiments are more susceptible, and her intellectual perceptions are truer and keener in respect to those matters requiring delicacy of taste and refinement of mind. Her humane sympathies are also stronger; she is sooner moved by the sentiments of compassion, benevolence, and charity. Blessings on her gentle heart! What a dreary world would this be without woman! And it is only polygamy that appreciates and appropriates her. Monogamy neglects her, spurns her, corrupts her, and degrades her.

IF A MAN MAY HAVE A PLURALITY OF WIVES, WHY
MAY NOT A WOMAN HAVE A PLURALITY OF HUS-
BANDS?

Because a woman's heart is so constituted, that
it is impossible for her to cherish a sincere love for
more than one husband at the same time. It is
even difficult for her to believe that a man can
cherish a sincere and honest love for more than one
woman at the same time. It is difficult for her to
believe it; for she cannot comprehend it. Her own
instincts revolt against the thought of a plurality of
husbands, and, judging his feeling by her own, she
does not see how a man can want, or at least can
truly love, a plurality of wives. But, as this point
involves a constitutional difference of sex, it is one
in which we must be aware that our feelings cannot guide us. A man can never know the infinite
tenderness and the infinite patience of a mother's
love, except imperfectly, by reason and observation. His experience does not teach him. His
paternal love does not exactly resemble it. So a
woman can never know the purity and sincerity of
a man's conjugal love for a plurality of wives, ex-

cept by similar observation and reason. Her conjugal love is unlike it. Her love for one man exhausts and absorbs her whole conjugal nature: there is no room for more. And if she ever receives the truth that his nature is capable of a plural love, she must attain it by the use of her reason, or admit it upon the testimony of honest men.

THE SUN AND THE PLANETS ; OR MARRIAGE LIKE GRAVITATION.

It would be as impossible and as unnatural for a pure-minded, virtuous woman to have more than one husband, as for the earth to have more than one sun ; but it is not unnatural nor impossible for a pure and noble-minded man to cherish the most devoted love for several wives at the same time : it is as natural for him as it is for the sun to have several planets at the same time, each one dependent on him, and each one harmonious in her own sphere. To each planet the sun yields all the light and heat which she is capable of receiving, or which she would be capable of receiving, were she the only planet in the sky. Each planet attracts the sun to the utmost of her weight, — the exhaustion of her power ; and the sun returns her attraction to an exactly equal degree, and no more. Not one planet nor two, nor all combined, are able to exhaust his power, or move him from his sphere. One more illustration : if a strong man holds one end of a cord, and a little child the other, and they pull towards each other, the tension of the cord is measured by the strength of the child, and not by that of the man. The same degree of power is felt at each end of the cord. The strength of the child is exhausted, that of the man is not. He can draw several children to him, sooner than they could unitedly draw him to them. A similar relation exists, naturally, between the male and the female. He is the sun, they are the planets. He is strong, they are weak. Let us not find fault with the ordinances of God, nor attempt to resist his will.

MASCULINE RESPONSIBILITY AND CARE.

The responsibilities of the man are in proportion to his strength and authority. He must assume the care and provide for the support of the family; and his female companions will submit to this authority, if they are wise and prudent, with all the grace and gentleness which distinguish their sex.

> " Thy husband is thy lord, thy life, thy keeper,
>   Thy head, thy sovereign; one that cares for thee
>   And for thy maintenance; commits his body
>   To painful labor, both by sea and land;
>   To watch the night in storms, the day in cold,
>   While thou liest warm at home, secure and safe;
>   And craves no other tribute at thy hands,
>   But love, fair looks, and true obedience, —
>   Too little payment for so great a debt.
>   Such duty as the subject owes the prince,
>   Even such a woman oweth to her husband;
>   And when she's froward, peevish, sullen, sour,
>   And not obedient to his honest will,
>   What is she but a foul contending rebel,
>   And graceless traitor to her loving lord?
>   I am ashamed that women are so simple
>   To offer war where they should kneel for peace;
>   Or seek for rule, supremacy, and sway,
>   When they are bound to serve, love, and obey.
>   Why are our bodies soft and weak and smooth,
>   Unapt to toil and trouble in the world;
>   But that our soft conditions and our hearts
>   Should well agree with our external parts? "
>   TAMING THE SHREW act v. scene ii.

The capacity of a man to attract and support several women must depend upon the amount of his talent, his fortune, and his benevolence, as well as upon his physical strength and vitality. There are some men who are scarcely able to attract the love and provide for the support of one woman; others are well able, if they were willing, to maintain several wives, but they are too penurious and too selfish to attempt it: and such men do not deserve the love of one. But there are others who are both able and willing, and who can as well love and provide for several as for one, and even better; for, if a man of immense vitality and corresponding mentality have but one, she must necessarily suffer from the superabundance of his power, and perhaps, like Semele in the too ardent embraces of Jove, may prove an early victim to the powerful demonstrations of his love. But even should he use the utmost tenderness, and never forget to restrain his burning ardor, yet, so long as he lives under the system of monogamy, such a husband must often be the occasion of the keenest suffering to a delicate woman. It is a source of constant pain and grief to her that she cannot come up to her husband's capacity, nor satisfy his conjugal requirements. She often tortures herself with the thought that he cannot love her, for she feels herself so much his inferior, and so utterly unworthy of his love. She often says that she knows he wishes her to die, that he might marry another. She wishes herself dead. She is madly jealous of every other woman who comes within the circle of their acquaintance, even though her husband may have no fancy for her; but the poor wife fears he may have, and this constant fear is worse than the worst reality. But, on the other hand, if he were a polygamist, and this same woman were one of his wives, she would then be happy and content. For she would continue to receive from him all the demonstrations of love she is capable of enduring, while she would joyfully contribute her share towards completing the capacity of his. Then it would constitute her happiness to behold him happy, and to enjoy the consciousness of having done what she could to make him so. She now *rejoices* in his abundant vitality, and *is proud* of his superiority. And when his manliness, his dignity, and his power are

radiated upon her beaming countenance, and re-
flected thence, it is then that her heart is filled with
the utmost delight and satisfaction of which it is
susceptible. Having become his wife, she is so
entirely devoted to him, that she almost loses in
him her own identity. She throws herself upon
his ample breast and within his infolding arms,
and yields both her person and her will to his
control ; and she only regrets, when she has given
up all, that she has not more to give.

> " You see me, Lord Bassanio, where I stand,
>   Such as I am ; though for myself alone
>   I would not be ambitious in my wish
>   To wish myself much better ; yet for you,
>   I would be trebled twenty times myself ;
>   A thousand times more fair, ten thousand times
>   More rich :
>   That only to stand high on your account,
>   I might, in virtues, beauties, livings, friends,
>   Exceed account ; but the full sum of me
>   Is an unlessoned girl, unschooled, unpractised ;
>   Happy in this, she is not yet so old
>   But she may learn ; and happier than this,
>   She is not bred so dull but she can learn ;
>   Happiest of all, is, that her gentle spirit
>   Commits itself to yours to be directed,
>   As from her lord, her governor, her king.

Myself and what is mine, to you and yours
Is now converted : but now I was the lord
Of this fair mansion, master of my servants,
Queen o'er myself; and even now, but now,
This house, these servants, and this same myself,
Are yours, my lord ; I give them with this ring.''

MERCHANT OF VENICE, act iii. scene ii.

APPENDIX.

WHEN this little book was ready for the press, I found, in one of our public libraries, an ancient work, in three volumes, on the same subject, with a formidable Greek title, as follows: " Thelyph-thora; or, a Treatise on Female Ruin, in its Causes, Effects, Consequences, Prevention, and Remedy," &c. Published by J. Dodsley. London, 1781. The work is learned and heavy, yet it passed through several editions, and had evidently attracted attention. The author's name does not appear; but it is well known to have been written by Rev. Martin Madan, D.D., Chaplain of the Lock Hospital, London; to the wardens and patrons of which the work is dedicated. I have read it with much interest, and find it to contain abundant confirmation of the views expressed in the foregoing pages.

224

In the preface to the second edition, the author says, " I now conclude this preface with the contents of a paper received from a very respectable clergyman, who was candid enough to let his prejudices submit to his judgment, and had honesty enough to own it."

I transcribe the greater part of that " paper," omitting such parts as apply to England only, and not to America.

" As the subject of a late publication entitled Thelyphthora, or a Treatise on Female Ruin, &c., is much misunderstood and misrepresented by many people, who have, some of them, never read it at all, and the rest but partially, and not without prejudice, and therefore oppose it, 'tis judged best to send its opposers the following questions for them to answer. The doing of this, 'tis thought, will bring the matter to a point, enter upon particulars, and be a means to discover where and with whom truth is, and where and with whom error is.

" 1. Are the mischievous, shocking crimes of whoredom, fornication, and adultery got to an enormous and increasing height in the land, and is the

land defiled and deluged by them, or not? and is
the frown of God upon the land, or is it not?

" 2. Is it needful, and is it our bounden duty, to
cry aloud against these God-provoking and nation-
ruining sins, and to seek a remedy against this
monstrous evil, or is it not?

" 3. Is there any thing destructively horrible in
the lives, and any thing shockingly dreadful in the
deaths, of abandoned women, *alias* common prostitutes, or is there not?

" 4. What number, how many thousands, are
there of these miserable creatures in our land? and
have they any evil effect on the male sex, or not?

" 5. Do our laws, as they now stand, hinder this
ruinous evil, or do they not? and can they, or can
they not?

" 8. Is there any remedy at all spoken of in
God's word against the great evil of lewdness?
and, if there be, what is that particular remedy?

" 9. Does God, in his word, order that whores,
adulterers, and adulteresses shall be put to death, or
does he not? (See Lev. xx. 10 ; Deut. xxii. 21, 22.)

" 12. Is there any particular recompense that
God in his word orders an unmarried man to make

to a virgin whom he has defiled, or is there not? and, if there be, what is it? (See Ex. xxii. 16, 17; Deut. xxii. 28, 29.)

." 13. Is there any particular recompense that a *married* man is enjoined to make the virgin whom he has defiled, or is there not? If there be, what is it? Is the virgin in the above case to receive a recompense, and the virgin in this case to receive none, and to be abandoned? (See the Scriptures above noted.)

" 14. Is our marriage-ceremony in the church so of the essence of marriage as to *constitute* marriage; and, therefore, none are married in God's sight, but what are joined together by a priest with that ceremony?

" 15. Is the marriage of the people called 'Quakers' in this land marriage in God's sight? and also according to our laws?

" 17. In what way, or by what form, were all those people of old joined together, whose marriages are recorded in Scripture history?

" 18. In what way, or by what form, were Christians married for upwards of a thousand years immediately after the birth of Christ?

" 19. Was our church marriage-ceremony the consequence of Pope Innocent III. putting marriage, as a sacrament, into the hands of popish priests, or was it not?

" 20. What reason can be assigned for God's permitting so many people, and particularly some of his distinguished saints of old, to live allowedly in the practice of polygamy, and to die without ever reproving them, calling them to repentance, and without their ever expressing any sorrow for it, and showing any evidences at all of their repentance? and if God's word be the rule of our conduct, and if the example of these saints be written for our learning, what are we to learn from them respecting polygamy?

" 21. If these saints of old lived and died in *sin*, by living and dying in the allowed practice of polygamy, what is the *name* of the sin? By what term is it to be distinguished? Was it adultery? or whoredom? or fornication? Was their commerce licit, or illicit? What commandment did they sin against? Were they adulterers, whoremongers, or fornicators? What does the Scripture history of the lives and deaths of these saints teach us to call their practice?

" 22. Were Hannah and Rachel and (after Uriah's death) Bathsheba whores or adulteresses ; or were they lawful and honored wives? How are they spoken of, and how were they treated, as the Scripture history informs us?

" 23. Were Joseph, Samuel, and Solomon bastards, or honorable and legitimate sons? In what character were they spoken of and treated? Did God show favor to them, or dislike of them?

" 24. Were not Hannah, Rachel, and Bathsheba whores or adultresses ; and Joseph, Samuel, and Solomon bastards, according to the laws of our land?

" 26. In what way can a stop be put to these following ruinous, detestable, horrible, and national evils ; namely, brothel-keeping ; murdering of infants by seduced women ; pregnant virgins committing of suicides ; the venereal disease ; seduction ; prostitution ; whoredom ; adultery ; and all the deplorable evils accompanying and following the mischievous sins of lewdness in this land? If God's law respecting the commerce of the sexes was observed, and if the laws of our land were to enforce that, might we not expect his blessing on

such means used to accomplish so needed and so
desirable an end?

"After these questions are answered, in a plain,
fair, and scriptural manner, and the answers are
honest, free from paltry subterfuge and equivoca-
tion, we shall find out whether the scheme in that
book has a good or a bad tendency; whether to be
reprobated or received; and whether the friends
and abettors of it are friends or foes to their country, the cause of God, the temporal, spiritual, and
eternal welfare of their fellow-creatures?"

Another learned work, in two octavo volumes,
bearing directly upon my subject, has just now
(1869) been issued from the London press, entitled "History of European Morals, from Augustus to Charlemagne. By W. E. H. Lecky, M. A."

The preceding pages of "The History and Philosophy of Marriage" had all been stereotyped
before these elegant volumes came to hand; and
it is only in this appendix, and at this last moment,
that I can pass them under a brief review. Having spent fifteen years in the same field of study,
with a similar object in view, and being well
aware of the interest and importance of this de-

partment of history, I scarcely need to say I have read Mr. Lecky's work with a keen appreciation of its worth, which has increased with each successive page. I cannot express my sincere admiration of the rare skill and fidelity with which the author has elaborated his theories, grouped his facts, and collated his authorities; investing the usually dry and abstruse study of moral philosophy with so much of both pleasure and profit as to unite the amusement of romance to the instruction of authentic records. The plan of my own essay, to which this notice is appended, being much less voluminous, and less pretentious, I could not introduce so many citations as I often wished, — an inability which I need not now regret, since this work has appeared, to which I can and do hereby refer. And yet these volumes do not seem to be altogether complete. They are as remarkable for what they omit as for what they contain, and suggest the question, Whether the distinguished author be not too good a philosopher to be, at the same time, a very good historian? whether his fondness for speculation has not too often diverted his attention from a categorical description of the morals and manners of the numerous tribes, and the long periods of time embraced within the scope of his history? His profound disquisitions are models of excellence, as such, and are copiously illustrated by incontestable facts and authorities; but he does not give us enough such disquisitions to constitute together the history of the morals of the given period. His work consists rather of *some speculations on European morals* than a history of them during seven centuries. He gives us admirable monographs on the different schools of moral philosophy, on the Pagan persecutions, on stoicism, on neo-Platonism, on miracles, on chastity, on asceticism, on monachism, on the celibacy of the clergy, on abortion, on infanticide, and exposure of children, &c., which are all very good; but he gives us no similar sketches of the history of marriage, of divorce, of adultery, of prostitution, of monogamy, of polygamy, of Paganism, of Gnosticism, of Catholicism, of Mohammedanism, &c., each one of which forms an essential part of the history of European morals. His plan of philosophical disquisitions, also, interrupts and confounds all chronological order, and leaves no room for those biographical sketches of distinguished men, whose private lives give moral tone and character to the times in which they live, which we always look for in a work of history, and especially in a history of morals, and the want of which, in these volumes, will be esteemed, by some at least, as a serious defect.

It happens, curiously enough, that what Mr. Lecky has omitted, I have, in " The History and Philosophy of Marriage," in part supplied, perhaps in a less satisfactory manner, but with no less sincere an appreciation of the truth, which it belongs to history to disentangle and unfold.

In the first chapter of "The History of European Morals," the author seems to me to degrade the passion of love and the institution of marriage below their just rank in the scale of morals, and to attribute to a life of continence a higher sanctity than the facts which he cites can warrant. (I quote from p. 107, *et seq.*, vol. i.)

" We have," says he, " an innate, intuitive, instinctive perception, that there is something degrading in the sensual part of our nature ; something to which a feeling of shame is naturally attached; something that jars with our conception of perfect purity; something we could not with any propriety ascribe to an all-holy Being." "It is this feeling, or instinct, which produces that sense of the sanctity of perfect continence, which the Catholic Church has so warmly encouraged, but which may be traced through the most distant ages and the most various creeds. We find it among the Nazarenes and the Essenes of Judæa, among the priests of Egypt and India, in the monasteries of Tartary, and . . . in the mythologies of Asia." "In the midst of the sensuality of ancient Greece, chastity was the pre-eminent attribute ascribed to Athene and Artemis. 'Chaste daughter of Zeus,' prayed the suppliants in Æschylus, 'thou whose calm eye is never troubled, look down upon us! Virgin, defend the virgins!'" "Celibacy was an essential condition in a few orders of priests, and in several orders of priestesses." "Strabo mentions the existence in Thrace of societies of men aspiring to perfection by celibacy and austere lives." At Rome, . . . "we find the traces of this higher ideal in the intense sanctity attributed to the vestal virgins, . . . in the legend of Claudia, . . . in the prophetic gift so often attributed to virgins, in the law which sheltered them from an execution, and in the language of Statius, who described marriage itself as a fault. In Christianity, scarcely any other single circumstance has contributed so much to the attraction of the faith as the ascription of virginity to the female ideal."

Now, all this, and a deal more, which I need

not quote, of the same sort, only proves, that, in respect of chastity, they frequently adore it most who lack it most ; and, in respect of love and marriage, that human sentiments are so influenced by fashionable vice, that we are often ashamed of what we ought to be proud, and proud of what we ought to be ashamed. We possess such contradictory sentiments and such conflicting passions, that we need a divine law to teach us what is right and what is wrong, and what is pure and what is impure. And divine law has taught us that marriage is honorable ; that the normal exercise of love is the noblest and purest passion of the soul ; and that the normal gratification of the reproductive instinct is the highest function of the body : and those only are ashamed of it who either indulge it abnormally and sinfully, or who desire to. Then, by the law of association, this guilty impurity imparts its own defilement to every act and thought of love, until the passion itself seems, as it is to them, degrading and impure. Thus this notion arises, not from its proper use, but only from its abuse ; and the law of increase ever remains the primal law of Nature : nor is it true, as he as-

serts, that we cannot, with any propriety, ascribe
it to an " all-holy Being."   Our first parents were
" all-holy ;" yet this passion can be ascribed to
them with the utmost propriety ; for " God said
unto them, Be fruitful, and multiply, and replenish
the earth."   " And they were not ashamed."

> " Nor turned, I ween,
> Adam from his fair spouse ; nor Eve the rites
> Mysterious of connubial love refused :
> Whatever hypocrites austerely talk
> Of purity and place and innocence ;
> Defaming as impure what God declares
> Pure, and commands to some, leaves free to all."

But our author's own pages furnish further refutation of his theory, in his sketch of the history of
asceticism, which at the same time affords so
full and so apt a confirmation of my assertions in
respect of the evil influences of Gnosticism and
Platonism upon mediæval Christianity and the
European marriage-system, that I quote the following from his 4th and 5th chapters, vol. ii. pp.
108, 119, 138, 340, 363, &c. : —

" The central conceptions of the monastic system
are the meritoriousness of complete abstinence from

all sexual intercourse, and of complete renunciation of the world. The first of these notions appeared in the very earliest period, in the respect attached to the condition of virginity, which was always regarded as sacred, and especially esteemed in the clergy, though for a long time it was not imposed as an obligation." "On the outskirts of the Church, the many sects of Gnostics and Manicheans all held, under different forms, the essential evil of matter." "The object of the ascetic was to attract men to a life of virginity; and, as a necessary consequence, marriage was treated as an inferior state." "'To cut down by the axe of virginity the wood of marriage,' was, in the energetic language of St. Jerome, the end of the saint." "Whenever any strong religious fervour fell upon a husband or a wife, its first effect was to make a happy union impossible. The more religious partner immediately desired to live a life of solitary asceticism." "St. Nilus, when he had already two children, was seized with a longing for the prevailing asceticism; and his wife was persuaded, after many tears, to consent to their separation. St. Ammon, on the night of his marriage, proceeded to greet his bride with an harangue upon the evils of the married state, and they agreed at once to separate. St. Melania labored long and earnestly to induce her husband to allow her to desert his bed." "St. Abraham ran away from his wife on the night of his marriage." "Woman was represented as the door of hell, as the mother of all human ills. She should be ashamed at the very thought that she is a woman. She should live in continual penance, on account of the curses she has brought upon the

world. She should be ashamed of her dress ; for
it is the memorial of her fall. She should be especially ashamed of her beauty ; for it is the most
potent instrument of the demon." "To break by
his ingratitude the heart of the mother who had
borne him, to persuade the wife who adored him
that it was her duty to separate from him forever,
to abandon his children, was regarded by the hermit as the most acceptable offering he could make
to his God." "St. Simeon Stylites, who had been
passionately loved by his parents, began his saintly
career by breaking the heart of his father, who died
of grief at his flight to the desert. His mother,
twenty-seven years after, when she heard, for the
first time, where he was, hastened to visit him.
But all her labor was in vain : no woman was admitted within the precincts of his dwelling ; and he
refused to permit her even to look upon his face."
"Three days and three nights she wept and en-
treated in vain ; and exhausted with grief, age,
and privation, she sank feebly to the ground, and
breathed her last before his door. Then, for the
first time, the saint, accompanied by his followers,
came out. He shed some pious tears over the
corpse of his murdered mother, and offered up a
prayer, consigning her soul to heaven. Then,
amid the admiring murmurs of his disciples, the
saintly matricide returned to his devotions." "He
had bound a rope around him, so that it had become embedded in his flesh, which putrified around
it. A horrible stench exhaled from his body, and
worms dropped from him whenever he moved. He
built successively three pillars, the last being sixty
feet high, and scarcely three feet in circumference ;

and on this pillar he lived during thirty years, exposed to every change of climate, ceaselessly and rapidly bending his body in prayer almost to the level of his feet. For one year, he stood upon one leg, the other being covered with hideous ulcers; while his biographer was commissioned to stand by his side, and pick up the worms that fell from his body, and replace them in the sores, the saint saying to the worm, 'Eat what God has given you.'" "For six months, St. Macarius of Alexandria slept in a marsh, and exposed his body, naked, to the stings of venomous flies. He was accustomed to carry about with him eighty pounds of iron. His disciple, St. Eusebius, carried a hundred and fifty pounds of iron, and lived for three years in a dried-up well. St. Sabinus would only eat corn that had become rotten by remaining for a month in water." "A man named Mutius, accompanied by his only child, a little boy of eight years old, once abandoned his possessions, and demanded admission into a monastery. The monks received him; but they proceeded to discipline his heart. His little child was clothed in rags, beaten, spurned, and ill treated. Day after day, the father was compelled to look upon his boy wasting away in sorrow, his once happy countenance forever stained with tears, distorted by sobs of anguish. But yet, says the admiring biographer, such was his love for Christ, and for the virtue of obedience, that the father's heart was rigid and unmoved."

"But most terrible of all were the struggles of young and ardent men, through whose veins the hot blood of passion continually flowed, physically incapable of a life of celibacy, who were borne on the wave of enthusiasm to the desert life. In the arms of Syrian or African brides, whose soft eyes answered love with love, they might have sunk to rest; but in the lonely desert no peace could ever visit their souls. Multiplying, with frantic energy, the macerations of the body, beating their breasts with anguish, the tears forever streaming from their eyes, imagining themselves continually haunted by forms of deadly beauty, their struggles not unfrequently ended in insanity and in suicide. When St. Pachomius and St. Palæmon were once conversing together in the desert, a young monk rushed into their presence in a distracted manner, and, convulsed with sobs, poured out his tale of sorrows. A woman had entered his cell, and had seduced him, and then vanished, leaving him half dead upon the ground; then, with a wild shriek, the monk broke away, rushed across the desert till he arrived at the next village; and there, leaping into the open furnace of the public baths, he perished in the flames."

" In the time of St. Cyprian, before the Decian persecution, it had been common to find clergy professing celibacy, but keeping, under various pretexts, their mistresses in their houses; and, after Constantine, the complaints on this subject became loud and general. Virgins and monks often lived together in the same house; and with a curious audacity of hypocrisy, which is very frequently noticed, they professed to have so overcome the passions of their nature, that they shared in chastity the same bed." " Noble ladies, pretending a desire to live a life of continence, abandoned their husbands, to live with low-born lovers. Palestine, which soon became the centre of pilgrimages, had become, in the time of St. Gregory of Nyssa, a hot-bed of debauchery." "There were few towns in Central Europe, on the way to Rome, in the eighth century, where English ladies who started as pilgrims were not living in open prostitution."

The last chapter of this "History of European Morals" also furnishes a complete confirmation of my own assertion (*ante* p. 60), that the barbarian polygamists from Asia, who successively invaded Europe, were possessed of a higher social purity than the monogamous Romans, or than they themselves possessed after they had adopted the European system.

"In respect of this virtue [chastity], the various tribes of barbarians, however violent and lawless, were far superior to the more civilised community." "The moral purity of the barbarians was of a kind altogether different from that which the ascetic movement inculcated. It was concentrated exclusively upon marriage. It showed itself in a noble conjugal fidelity; but it was little fitted for a life of celibacy." "The practice of polygamy among the barbarian kings was also, for some centuries, unchecked, or, at least, unsuppressed, by Christianity. The kings Caribert and Chilperic had both many wives at the same time. Clothaire married the sister of his first wife during the lifetime of the latter; who, on the king announcing

16

his intention to her, is reported to have said, ' Let my lord do what seemeth good in his sight; only let thy servant live in thy favour.' St. Columbanus was expelled from Gaul chiefly on account of his denunciations of the polygamy of King Thierry. Dagobert had three wives, as well as a multitude of concubines. Charlemagne himself had, at the same time, two wives ; and he indulged largely in concubines. After this period, examples of this nature became rare." " But, notwithstanding these startling facts, there can be no doubt that the general purity of the barbarians was, from the first, superior to that of the later Romans."

Perhaps our learned author calls these facts " startling," because they do not accord with modern notions of the superior purity of monogamy which he seems to entertain, in common with other Europeans, in spite of a thousand other " facts " to the contrary which his own volumes contain. For example, in his sketch of the morals of ancient Greece, the " facts " seem " perplexing " to him. In the heroic age, when polygamy was practised, the noblest types of female virtue and excellence abounded ; but in the later period, when the " higher state " of monogamy prevailed, female virtue experienced a sudden eclipse, so dark and total, and so incompatible with his theory of the superior purity of monogamy, that he expresses the utmost shame and reluctance in being obliged to record the evidences of its gross depravity. Hear what he says, and pardon his errors in theory, for they are those of his age; admire his candor, and fidelity to facts, for they are the highest qualifications of an historian.

"It is one of the most remarkable, and, to some writers, one of the most perplexing facts in the moral history of Greece, that, in the former and ruder period, women had undoubtedly the highest place, and their type exhibited the highest perfection. Moral ideas, in a thousand forms, have been sublimated, enlarged, and changed by advancing civilisation; but it may be fearlessly asserted, that the types of female excellence which are contained in the Greek poems, while they are among the earliest, are also among the most perfect, in the literature of mankind. The conjugal tenderness of Hector and Andromache; the unwearied fidelity of Penelope, awaiting through the long, revolving years the return of her storm-tossed husband; the heroic love of Alcestis, voluntarily dying, that her husband might live; the filial piety of Antigone; the majestic grandeur of the death of Polyxena; the more saintly resignation of Iphigenia, excusing with her last breath the father who had condemned her; the joyous, modest, and loving Nausicaa, whose figure shines like a perfect idyll among the tragedies of the Odyssey, — all these are pictures of perennial beauty which Rome and Christendom, chivalry and modern civilisation, have neither eclipsed nor transcended. Virgin modesty and conjugal fidelity, the graces as well as the virtues of the most perfect womanhood, have never been more exquisitely pourtrayed."

Such was the golden age of polygamy. Now look on that picture, and then on this, both drawn by the same hand, and that the hand of a monogamist.

" In the historical [or monogamous] age of Greece, the legal position of women had, in some measure, slightly improved; but their moral condition had undergone a marked deterioration. The foremost and most dazzling type of Ionic womanhood was the courtesan; and among the males, at least, the empire of passion was almost unrestricted. The peculiarity of Greek sensuality is, that it grew up, for the most part, uncensured, and, indeed, even encouraged, under the eyes of some of the most illustrious of moralists. If we can imagine Ninon de l'Enclos, at a time when the rank and splendour of Parisian society thronged her drawing-rooms, reckoning a Bossuet or a Fénelon among her followers; if we can imagine these prelates publicly advising her about her profession, and the means of attaching the affections of her lovers, — we shall have conceived a relation like that which existed between Socrates and the courtesan Theodota." " In the Greek civilisation, legislators and moralists recognised two distinct orders of womanhood,

— the wife, whose first duty was fidelity to her husband, and the hetæra, the mistress, who subsisted by her fugitive attachments. The wives lived in almost absolute seclusion. They were usually married when very young. The more wealthy seldom went abroad, and never, except when accompanied by a female slave; never attended the public spectacles; received no male visitors, except in the presence of their husbands; and had not even a seat at their own tables when male guests were there. Thucydides doubtless expressed the prevailing sentiment of his countrymen when he said that the highest merit of woman is not to be spoken of either for good or for evil." "The names of virtuous women scarcely appear in Greek history." "A few instances of conjugal and filial affection have been recorded; but, in general, the only women who attracted the notice of the people were the hetæræ, or courtesans." "The voluptuous worship of Aphrodite gave a kind of religious sanction to their profession. Courtesans were the priestesses in her temples." "The courtesan was the queen of beauty. She was the model of the statues of Aphrodite, that commanded the admiration of Greece. Praxiteles was accustomed to reproduce the form of Phyrne; and her statue, carved in gold, stood in the temple of Apollo." "Apelles was at once the painter and lover of Lais." "The courtesan was the one free woman of Athens; and she often availed herself of her freedom to acquire a degree of knowledge which enabled her to add to her other charms an intense intellectual fascination." . . . "My task in describing this aspect of Greek life has been an eminently

unpleasing one; and I should certainly not have
entered upon even the baldest and most guarded
disquisition on a subject so difficult, painful, and
delicate, had it not been absolutely indispensable to
a history of morals. What I have written will
sufficiently explain why Greece, which was fertile,
probably, beyond all other lands, in great men, was
so remarkably barren of great women." "The Christian doctrine, that it is criminal to gratify a powerful and a transient physical appetite, except under
the condition of a lifelong contract, was altogether
unknown." "An aversion to marriage became
very general, and illicit connections were formed
with the most perfect frankness and publicity."

In support of his opinion, that monogamy is
a higher state of morals than polygamy, Mr.
Lecky, in the final chapter, brings forward four
arguments, which merit a fair statement.

"We may regard monogamy," he says, "either
in the light of our intuitive moral sentiment on the
subject of chastity, or in the light of the interests
of society. By the first, I understand that universal perception or conviction which I believe to be
an ultimate fact in human nature, that the sensual
side of our being is the lower side, and some degree
of shame may appropriately be attached to it. In its
Oriental or polygamous stage, marriage is regarded
almost exclusively in its sensual aspect, as a gratification of the animal passions; while in European
marriages . . . the lower element has compara-

tively little prominence. In this respect, it may
be intelligibly said that monogamy is a higher state
than polygamy. The utilitarian arguments are
also extremely powerful, and may be summed up
in three sentences. Nature, by making the number of males and females nearly equal, indicates it
as natural. In no other form of marriage can the
government of the family be so happily sustained;
and in no other does woman assume the position
of the equal of man."

I have already anticipated and considered the last
three arguments in " The History and Philosophy
of Marriage," and I have also incidentally touched
upon the first in my examination of our author's
views of chastity and continence; but, as he seems
to place great stress upon this notion, and repeats
it again and again, I will venture to offer another
word in reply. If an enforced monogamy be more
chaste than polygamy, then, for a stronger reason,
an enforced celibacy is more chaste than monogamy, — a conclusion of which his own work
demonstrates the absurdity, as does every other
respectable history of real life in any age or country. I yield to no one in a most profound respect
for chastity, and in a most sincere desire to promote it; but by as much as I venerate true chas-

tity by so much do I detest its counterfeit. I have demonstrated that our present system of monogamy is a counterfeit, stimulating the most loathsome vices of prostitution and hypocrisy; and I assert that the only effectual manner in which social purity and honesty can be maintained is by promoting the utmost freedom to marry, and the utmost purity of marriage. All men are not alike. Let there be no Procustean marriage-bed. If there are those who are able and willing, for the love of God and the better service of the Church, to devote themselves to a voluntary life of honest celibacy, we respect and venerate them for it. If there are others who will each honestly and cheerfully content himself with one wife, " and, forsaking all others, keep himself only unto her so long as they both shall live," at the same time avoiding all matrimonial abuse and excess, we will respect them but little less than the former; but, again, if there are others, whose measure of vitality is so large that they cannot and will not be restricted to a single marriage, or whose wives are confirmed invalids, and hopelessly barren and incapable of matrimonial duty, — I would not oblige these men either to murder or to divorce their present wives, or to live a life of matrimonial brutality, or of desperate licentiousness; but I would grant them the right to marry again, as the best possible alternative. And I insist that the man who should thus openly maintain his natural rights, and live an honest life, would still be worthy of public confidence and respect. Such men, by taking additional wives, would become the most efficient public benefactors, by providing for the otherwise homeless and abandoned women, and by furnishing the only possible preventive of the great social evil. The time has gone by for accepting the mere outward profession of sanctity: we require substantial evidences of its possession before we consent to accord to its claimants their proper honors. No one can now escape publicity. The almost omnipresent reporters of the press invade our sanctuaries and our bedchambers; and a bird of the air shall carry the matter. Men and women need affect no purity or sanctity which they do not possess. The fiat has gone forth, "Let there be light;" and, in our present situation, what we most desire is more light. And Mr. Lecky himself, at last, virtually admits, that, while monogamy should be the ideal type of the matrimonial relation, its universal, honest observance is an impossibility. But, instead of recommending the pure and divinely-sanctioned freedom of polygamy, he prefers to pander to the licentious tendencies of a luxurious age, by suggesting the alternative of loose connections with temporary mistresses.

" The life-long union," says he, " of one man and of one woman should be the normal or dominant type of intercourse between the sexes." " But it by no means follows, that, because it should be the dominant type, it should be the only one, or that the interests of society demand that all connections should be forced into the same die. Connections which are confessedly only for a few years have always subsisted side by side with permanent marriages ; and in periods when public opinion, acquiescing in their propriety, inflicts no excommunication on one or both of the partners when these partners are not living the demoralising and degrading life which accompanies the consciousness of guilt, and when proper provision is made for the children who are born, it would be, I believe, impossible to prove, by the light of simple and unassisted reason, that such connections should be invariably condemned. It is extremely important, both for the happiness and for the moral well-being of men, that life-long unions should not be effected simply under the prompting of a blind appetite. There are always multitudes, who, in the period of their lives when their passions are most strong, are incapable of supporting children in their own social rank, and who would therefore injure society by marrying in it, but are, nevertheless, perfectly capable of securing an honorable career for their illegitimate children in the lower social sphere to which they would naturally belong. Under the conditions I have mentioned, these connections are not injurious, but beneficial, to the weaker partner ; they soften the differences of rank, they stimulate social habits, and they do not produce upon character the degrading effect of promiscuous intercourse, or upon society the injurious effects of imprudent marriages, one or the other of which will multiply in their absence. In the immense variety of circumstances and characters, cases will always appear in which, on utilitarian grounds, they might seem advisable."

Thus, at last, this fashionable vice has lifted the mask of hypocrisy a little, and found a voice, and spoken for itself. And I have given ample space and full expression to these arguments for monogamy, of which this form of prostitution, or some worse one, is a necessary part, requesting my opponents to reciprocate this favor of placing their arguments side by side with mine, and entreating the Public to judge between them, and, before awarding judgment, to be sure to *hear the other side.* If there is any truth in the Holy Bible, it teaches the innocence of polygamy, and the sinfulness of every form of sexual indulgence not guarded by a life-long marriage. If there is any truth in history, it teaches the innate impurity of enforced monogamy, — an impurity which has always increased with the increase of wealth and the advance of civilization; which perverted Christianity itself is powerless to prevent; which has corrupted and wasted many nations; and into which we are drifting with inevitable certainty, and from which nothing but an extension of the benefits and the safeguards of marriage can ever deliver us, — all which propositions are demonstrated in " The History and Philosophy of Marriage."

I beg leave to refer, also, to a recent work entitled " An Historical Sketch of Sacerdotal Celibacy in the Christian Church. By H. C. Lea." Philadelphia: J. B. Lippincott & Co., 1867.

This is a valuable repertory of authentic recorded facts, cited from

"Many a quaint and curious volume of forgotten lore,"

confirming the views advanced in " The History

and Philosophy of Marriage" in respect of the degrading influences of the Roman system of restricted marriage, from which I have proved our European monogamy to have been derived. I earnestly commend this book to the attention of every student of moral philosophy, and to that of every Christian philanthropist.

Conybeare and Howson's "Life and Epistles of St. Paul" contains the following note on 1 Tim. iii. 2, concerning the "one wife" of a bishop, which I place alongside of Dr. McKnight's (page 72). It also confirms my own statements in the chapter on the origin of monogamy.

"In the corrupt facility of divorce allowed both by the Greek and Roman law, it was very common for man and wife to separate, and marry other parties, during the life of one another. Thus a man might have three or four living wives; or rather women who had all successively been his wives. . . . A similar code is [now] unhappily to be found in Mauritius; there . . . it is not uncommon to meet in society three or four women who have all been the wives of the same man. . . . We believe it is this kind of *successive* polygamy, rather than *simultaneous* polygamy, which is here spoken of as disqualifying for the Presbyterate. So Beza."

INDEX.

Other Books Published by Don Milton

Title	Author	Availability
Prince of Sumba Husband to Many Wives	Don Milton	Now
Letters to Joseph Priestley	Martin Madan	Now
Exhortatory Address to the Brethren in the Faith of Christ	Martin Madan	Soon
Thelyphthora Volume I A Treatise on Female Ruin	Martin Madan	Now
Thelyphthora Volume II A Treatise on Female Ruin	Martin Madan	Now
Thelyphthora Volume III A Treatise on Female Ruin	Martin Madan	Now
Thoughts on Executive Justice	Martin Madan	Soon
John Milton on Polygamy	John Milton	Soon
Many More Titles	Don Milton & Others	Spring 2010

To Purchase Books or to Contact Don Milton
Visit - DonMilton.com

www.ingramcontent.com/pod-product-compliance
Lightning Source LLC
Chambersburg PA
CBHW021858020426
42334CB00013B/381